# baby names
## and star signs book

part of the

package

UK £2.95   ISBN 1–84205–280–2

# baby names
## and star signs book

This edition published 2003 for D. C. Thomson & Co., Ltd. by
Geddes & Grosset.

© 2003 Geddes & Grosset.
David Dale House, New Lanark ML11 9DJ

**Aadesh** message (Indian).
**Aaron** mountaineer, enlightener (Hebrew); a contracted diminutive is *Arn*.
**Abbott** a surname, meaning father of the abbey, used as a first name (Old English).
**Abed** worshipper (Indian).
**Abel** breath, fickleness, vanity (Hebrew).
**Abdul-Baari** servant of the Creator (Indian).
**Abdul-Qudoos** servant of the Most Holy (Indian).
**Abhay** fearless (Indian).
**Abihu** to whom Jehovah is a father (Hebrew).
**Abijah** to whom Jehovah is a father (Hebrew); a diminutive form is *Bije*.
**Abraham** father of a multitude (Hebrew); diminutive forms are *Abe, Bram*.
**Abram** father of elevation (Hebrew); diminutive forms are *Abe, Bram*.
**Absalom** my father is peace (Hebrew).
**Ackley** a surname, meaning from the oak tree meadow, used as a first name (Old English).
**Adair** a Scottish form of *Edgar*.
**Adalard** noble and brave (Germanic).

**Adam** man, earth man, red earth (Hebrew).
**Addison** a surname, meaning Adam's son, used as a first name (Old English).
**Adin** sensual (Hebrew).
**Adlai** God is just (Hebrew).
**Adler** eagle, perceptive one (Germanic).
**Adney** island-dweller (Old English).
**Adolph, Adolphus** noble wolf; noble hero (Germanic); a diminutive form is *Dolph*.
**Adrian** of the Adriatic in Italy (Latin); a variant form is *Hadrian*.
**Adriel** from God's congregation (Hebrew).
**Aeneas** commended (Greek); a variant form is *Eneas*.
**Ahern** horse lord, horse owner (Irish Gaelic).
**Aidan** fire, flame (Irish Gaelic); a variant form is *Edan*.
**Aiken** the Scottish form of Atkin, a surname meaning son of Adam, used as a first name (Old English).
**Ainsley** a surname, meaning meadow of the respected one, used as a first name (Old English).
**Ainslie** a Scottish form of *Ainsley*, used as a first name.

3

**Alan** meaning uncertain, possibly a hound (Slavonic), harmony (Celtic); variant forms are *Allan, Allen*.

**Albern** noble warrior (Old English).

**Albert** all-bright; illustrious (Germanic); diminutive forms are *Al, Bert, Bertie*.

**Alcott** the surname, meaning old cottage or hut, used as a first name (Old English).

**Alden** a surname, meaning old or trustworthy friend, used as a first name (Old English).

**Alder** a surname, meaning alder tree, used as a first name (Old English); old, wise and rich (Germanic).

**Aldis** a surname, meaning old house, used as a first name (Old English).

**Aldo, Aldous** old (Germanic).

**Aldrich** a surname, meaning old, wise ruler, used as a first name (Old English).

**Aldwin** see Alvin.

**Alec, Aleck** diminutive forms of *Alexander*.

**Aled** the name of a river used as a first name (Welsh).

**Aleron** eagle (Latin).

**Alexander** a helper of men (Greek); diminutive forms are *Alec, Alex, Alick, Lex, Sandy*.

**Alexis** help; defence (Greek).

**Alfred** good or wise counsellor (Germanic); diminutive forms are *Alf, Alfie*.

**Alger** elf spear (Old English).

**Algernon** whiskered (Old French); a diminutive form is *Algie, Algy*.

**Alick** diminutive of *Alexander*, now used independently.

**Alister** the Scots Gaelic form of *Alexander*; variant forms are *Alasdair, Alastair*.

**Allard** noble and brave (Old English); a variant form is Alard.

**Almo** noble and famous (Old English).

**Alonso** a Spanish form of *Alphonso*; a diminutive form is *Lonnie*.

**Aloysius** a Latin form of Lewis.

**Alpha** first one (Greek).

**Alpheus** exchange (Hebrew).

**Alpin** blond (Scottish Gaelic).

**Alroy** red-haired (Scottish Gaelic).

**Alston** a surname, meaning old stone, used as a first name (Old English).

**Altman** old, wise man (Germanic).

**Alton** a surname, meaning old stream or source, used as a first name (Old English).

**Alvin, Alwin** winning all (Old English).

**Amadeus** lover of God (Latin).

**Amariah** whom Jehovah promised (Hebrew).

4

**Amasa** a burden (Hebrew).

**Ambert** shining bright light (Germanic).

**Ambrose** immortal (Greek).

**Amerigo** an Italian variant form of *Enrico*.

**Ammon** hidden (Egyptian).

**Amory** famous ruler (Germanic); variant forms are *Amery, Emery, Emmery*.

**Amos** bearer of a burden (Hebrew).

**Anastasius** form of *Anastasia*.

**Anatole** from the East (Greek).

**André** the French form of *Andrew*, becoming popular as an English-language form.

**Andreas** Greek, Latin, and German forms of *Andrew*.

**Andrew** strong; manly; courageous (Greek); diminutive forms are *Andy, Drew*.

**Aneirin, Aneurin** noble, modest (Welsh); a diminutive form is *Nye*.

**Angelo** Italian form of *Angel*.

**Angus** excellent virtue (Gaelic); a diminutive form is *Gus*.

**Anselm, Ansel** a surname, meaning, god helmet, i.e. under the protection of God, used as a first name (Germanic).

**Ansley** a surname, meaning clearing with a hermitage or solitary dwelling, used as a first name (Old English).

**Anson** a surname, meaning son of Agnes or Anne, used as a first name (Old English).

**Antony** priceless; praiseworthy (Latin); variant forms are *Anthony, Anton, Antoine, Antonio;* a diminutive form is *Tony*.

**Anwell** beloved (Gaelic).

**Anyon** anvil (Gaelic).

**Aonghas** Scots Gaelic form of *Angus*.

**Archard** sacred and powerful (Germanic).

**Archer** a surname, meaning professional or skilled bowman, used as a first name (Old English).

**Archibald** very bold; holy prince (Germanic); diminutive forms are *Archie, Archy*.

**Ardal** high valour (Irish Gaelic).

**Ardley** from the domestic meadow (Old English).

**Argus** all-seeing, watchful one, from Argus Panoptes, a character from Greek mythology with a hundred eyes all over his body (Greek).

**Argyle, Argyll** the Scottish placename, meaning land or district of the Gaels, used as a first name (Scots Gaelic).

**Aric** sacred ruler (Old English); diminutive forms are *Rick, Rickie, Ricky*.

**Arlen** pledge (Irish Gaelic).

**Armand** a French form of *Herman*.

**Armel** stone prince or chief (Breton Gaelic).

**Armin** military man (Germanic).

**Armstrong** a surname, meaning strong in the arm, used as a first name (Old English).

**Arnall** a surname variant form of *Arnold* used as a first name (Germanic).

**Arnatt, Arnett** surname variant forms of *Arnold* used as first names.

**Arnaud, Arnaut** French forms of *Arnold*.

**Arne** eagle (Old Norse); a diminutive form is *Arnie*.

**Arnold** strong as an eagle (Germanic); eagle meadow (Old English); diminutive forms are *Arn, Arnie, Arno, Arny*.

**Arnott** a surname variant form of *Arnold* used as a first name.

**Arnulf** eagle wolf (Germanic); diminutives are *Arn, Arno*.

**Artemas** form of *Artemis* (Greek).

**Arthur** eagle Thor (Celtic); a diminutive form is *Art*.

**Arturo** the Italian and Spanish forms of *Arthur*.

**Arval, Arvel** greatly lamented (Latin).

**Arvid** eagle wood (Norse).

**Arvin** people's friend (Germanic).

**Arwel** meaning uncertain (Welsh).

**Arwyn** muse (Welsh); a variant form is *Awen*.

**Asa** healer, physician (Hebrew).

**Asahel** made of God (Hebrew).

**Asaph** a collector (Hebrew).

**Ashley, Ashleigh** the surname, meaning ash wood or glade, used as a first name (Old English).

**Ashlin** ash-surrounded pool (Old English).

**Ashton** an English placename, meaning ash-tree farmstead, used as a first name (Old English).

**Ashur** martial, warlike (Semitic).

**Athanasius** immortal (Greek).

**Atherton** a surname, meaning noble army's place, used as a first name (Old English).

**Athol, Atholl** a placename and surname, meaning new Ireland, used as a first name (Scots Gaelic).

**Auberon** noble bear (Germanic); a variant form is Oberon; a diminutive form is *Bron*.

**Aubin** a surname, meaning blond one, used as a first name (French).

**Aubrey** ruler of spirits (Germanic).

# B

**Baahir** dazzling (Indian).

**Badal** cloud (Hindu).

**Bailey, Baillie** a surname, meaning bailiff or steward, used as a first name (Old French); a variant form is *Bayley*.

**Bainbridge** a surname, meaning bridge over a short river, used as a first name (Old English).

**Baird** a Scottish surname, meaning minstrel or bard, used as a first name (Celtic); a variant form is *Bard*.

**Balavan** powerful (Hindu).

**Baldwin** bold friend (Germanic).

**Balfour** a surname from a Scottish placename, meaning village with pasture, used as a first name (Scots Gaelic).

**Ballard** a surname, meaning bald, used as a first name (Old English/Old French).

**Balthasar, Balthazar** Baal defend the king (Babylonian).

**Bancroft** a surname, meaning bean place, used as a first name (Old English).

**Barclay** a surname, meaning birch wood, used as a first name (Old English); variant forms are *Berkeley, Berkley*.

**Bardolph** bright wolf (Germanic).

**Barid** cloud (Indian).

**Barlow** a surname, meaning barley hill or barley clearing, used as a first name (Old English).

**Barnaby, Barnabas** son of consolation and exhortation (Hebrew); a diminutive form is *Barney*.

**Barnet, Barnett** a surname, meaning land cleared by burning, used as a first name (Old English).

**Barnum** a surname, meaning homestead of a warrior, used as a first name (Old English).

**Baron** the lowest rank of the peerage used as a first name (Old French); a variant form is *Barron*.

**Barratt, Barrett** a surname, meaning commerce or trouble or strife, used as a first name (Old French).

**Barry** spear (Irish Gaelic).

**Bartholomew** a warlike son (Hebrew); diminutive forms are *Bart, Bat*.

**Bartley** a surname, meaning a birch wood or clearing, used as a first name (Old English); a diminutive form is *Bart*.

**Barton** a surname, meaning farm or farmyard, used as a first name (Old English); a diminutive form is *Bart*.

**Basel** brave (Indian).

**Bashaar** bringer of glad tidings (Indian).

**Basil** kingly, royal (Greek).

**Batuk** boy (Indian).

**Baxter** a surname, meaning

baker, used as a first name (Old English).

**Beaufort** a surname, meaning beautiful stronghold, used as a first name (French); a diminutive form is *Beau*.

**Beaumont** a surname, meaning beautiful hill, used as a first name (French); a diminutive form is *Beau*.

**Bellamy** a surname, meaning handsome friend, used as a first name (Old French).

**Ben** a diminutive form of *Benedict, Benjamin*, also used independently.

**Benedict, Benedick** blessed (Latin); also *Bennet*; diminutives are *Ben, Bennie, Benny, Benito*.

**Benjamin** son of the right hand (Hebrew); diminutive forms are *Ben, Benjie, Bennie, Benny*.

**Benson** a surname, meaning son of Ben, used as a first name.

**Bentley** a surname from a Yorkshire placename, meaning woodland clearing where bent-grass grows, used as a first name (Old English).

**Beppe, Beppo** a diminutive form of *Giuseppe*, occasionally used independently.

**Bernard** strong or hardy bear (Germanic); also *Barnard*; diminutive forms are *Barney, Bernie*.

**Berthold** bright ruler (Germanic); variant forms are *Barthold, Bertold, Berthoud*; diminutive forms are *Bert, Bertie*.

**Bertram** bright; fair; illustrious (Germanic); a variant form is *Bartram*; diminutive forms are *Bert, Bertie*.

**Bevan** a surname, meaning son of Evan, used as a first name (Welsh); variant forms are *Beavan, Beaven, Bevin*.

**Beverley, Beverly** a placename, meaning beaver stream, used as a first name (Old English); a diminutive form is *Bev*.

**Bevis** bull (French).

**Bhaskar** sun (Indian).

**Bhudev** lord of the earth (Hindu).

**Bhupati** god of the earth (Indian).

**Bibek** conscience, discrimination (Indian).

**Bing** a surname, meaning a hollow, used as a first name (Germanic).

**Birch** a surname, from the birch tree, used as a first name (Old English); a variant form is *Birk*.

**Bishop** a surname, meaning one who worked in a bishop's household, used as a first name (Old English).

**Björn** bear (Old Norse).

**Blair** a placename and surname, meaning a plain, used as a first name (Scots Gaelic).

**Blaise** sprouting forth (French).

**Blake** pale or fair-complexioned (Old English).

**Bleddyn** wolf (Welsh).

**Blyth, Blythe** a surname, meaning cheerful and gentle, used as a first name (Old English).

**Boas, Boaz** fleetness (Hebrew).

**Bonar** a surname, meaning gentle, kind, courteous, used as a first name (French); variant forms are *Bonnar, Bonner*.

**Boniface** doer of good (Latin).

**Booth** a surname, meaning hut or shed, used as a first name (Old Norse).

**Boris** small (Russian).

**Botolf, Botolph** herald wolf (Old English).

**Bowie** a surname, meaning yellow-haired, used as a first name (Scots Gaelic).

**Boyce** a surname, meaning a wood, used as a first name (Old French).

**Boyd** a surname, meaning light-haired, used as a first name (Scots Gaelic).

**Bradford** a placename and surname, meaning place at the broad ford, used as a first name (Old English).

**Bradley** a surname, meaning broad clearing or broad wood, used as a first name (Old English); a diminutive form is *Brad*.

**Brady** a surname, of unknown meaning, used as a first name (Irish Gaelic).

**Braham** a surname, meaning house or meadow with broom bushes, used as a first name.

**Bramwell** a surname, meaning from the bramble spring, used as a first name (Old English).

**Brand** firebrand (Old English).

**Brandon** a surname, meaning broom-covered hill, used as a first name (Old English); a variant form of *Brendan*.

**Brendan** prince (Celtic); a variant form is *Brandon*.

**Brent** a surname, meaning a steep place, used as a first name (Old English).

**Bret, Brett** a Breton (Old French).

**Brewster** a surname, meaning brewer, used as a first name (Old English).

**Brian** strong (Celtic); a variant form is *Bryan*.

**Brijesh** Lord Krishna (Indian).

**Bryce**, a surname of unknown meaning, used as a first name (Celtic).

**Broderic, Broderick** a surname, meaning son of Roderick, used as a first name (Welsh); brother (Scots Gaelic).

**Brodie, Brody** a surname, meaning ditch, used as a first name (Scots Gaelic).

**Brook, Brooke** a surname, meaning stream, used as a first name; a variant form is *Brooks*.

**Bruce** a surname, meaning unknown, used as a first name (Old French).

**Bruno** brown (Germanic).

**Bryn** hill (Welsh).

**Buck** stag; he-goat; a lively young man (Old English).

**Buckley** a surname, meaning stag or he-goat meadow, used as a first name (Old English).

**Budd, Buddy** the informal term for a friend or brother used as a first name (Old English).

**Burford** a surname, meaning ford by a castle, used as a first name (Old English).

**Burgess** a surname, meaning citizen or inhabitant of a borough, used as a first name (Old French).

**Burhaan** proof (Indian).

**Burn, Burne** a surname, meaning brook or stream, used as a first name (Old English); variant forms are *Bourn, Bourne, Byrne*.

**Burnett** a surname, meaning brown-complexioned or brown-haired, used as a first name (Old French).

**Burton** a surname, meaning farmstead of a fortified place, used as a first name (Old English); a diminutive form is *Burt*.

**Buster** an informal term of address for a boy or young man, now used as a first name (English).

**Byron** a surname, meaning at the cowsheds, used as a first name (Old English).

# C

**Cadell** a surname, meaning battle spirit, used as a first name (Welsh).

**Cadmus** man from the east; in mythology a Phoenician prince who founded Thebes with five warriors he had created (Greek).

**Caesar** long-haired; the Roman title of emperor used as a first name (Latin).

**Cain** possession; the Biblical character who killed his brother Abel (Hebrew).

**Calder** a placename and surname, meaning hard or rapid water, used as a first name (Celtic).

**Caldwell** a surname, meaning cold spring or stream, used as a first name (Old English).

**Caleb** a dog (Hebrew); a diminutive form is *Cale*.

**Calhoun** a surname, meaning from the forest, used as a first name (Irish Gaelic).

**Callisto** most fair or good (Greek).

**Calum, Callum** the Scots Gaelic form of *Columba*, the Latin for dove; a diminutive form of *Malcolm*; diminutive forms are *Cally, Caley*.

**Calvert** a surname, meaning calf herd, used as a first name (Old English).

**Calvin** little bald one (Latin).

**Cameron** a surname, meaning hook nose, used as a first name (Scots Gaelic).

**Campbell** a surname, meaning crooked mouth, used as a first name (Scots Gaelic).

**Canice** handsome or fair one (Irish Gaelic).

**Canute** knot (Old Norse), the name of a Danish king of England (1016-35); variant forms are *Cnut, Knut*.

**Caradoc, Caradog** beloved (Welsh); a variant form is *Cradoc*.

**Cardew** a surname meaning black fort, used as a first name (Welsh).

**Carey** a surname, meaning castle dweller (Welsh) or son of the dark one (Irish Gaelic), used as a first name; a variant form of *Cary*.

**Carl** an anglicized German and Swedish form of *Charles*.

**Carlton** a placename and surname, meaning farm of the churls — a rank of peasant, used as a first name (Old English); variant forms are *Carleton, Charlton, Charleton*; a diminutive form is *Carl*.

**Carmichael** a Scottish placename and surname, meaning fort of Michael, used as a first name (Celtic).

**Carr** a placename and surname, meaning overgrown marshy ground, used as a first name (Old Norse); variant forms are *Karr, Kerr*.

**Carrick** a placename, meaning rock, used as a first name (Gaelic).

**Carson** a surname, of uncertain meaning but possibly marsh dweller (Old English), used as a first name.

**Carter** a surname, meaning a driver or maker of carts (Old English), or son of Arthur (Scots Gaelic), used as a first name.

**Carver** great rock (Cornish Gaelic); a surname, meaning sculptor, used as a first name (Old English).

**Carwyn** blessed love (Welsh).

**Cary** a surname, meaning pleasant stream, used as a first name (Celtic); a variant form is *Carey*.

**Casey** an Irish surname, meaning vigilant, used as a first name; a placename, Cayce in

Kentucky, where the hero Casey Jones was born, used as a first name.

**Cashel** a placename, meaning circular stone fort, used as a first name (Irish Gaelic).

**Caspar, Casper** the Dutch form of *Jasper*, now also used as an English-language form.

**Cassian, Cassius** a Roman family name, of uncertain meaning – possibly empty, used as a first name (Latin); a diminutive form is *Cass*.

**Cassidy** a surname, meaning clever, used as a first name (Irish Gaelic); a diminutive form is *Cass*.

**Castor** beaver (Greek).

**Cathal** battle ruler (Irish Gaelic).

**Cato** a Roman family name, meaning wise one, used as a first name (Latin).

**Cavan** a placename, meaning hollow with a grassy hill, used as a first name (Irish Gaelic); a variant form is *Kavan*.

**Cecil** dim-sighted (Latin).

**Cedric** a name adapted by Sir Walter Scott for a character in Ivanhoe from the Saxon Cerdic, the first king of Wessex.

**Ceinwen** beautiful and blessed (Welsh).

**Cephas** a stone (Aramaic).

**Chad** meaning uncertain – possibly warlike, bellicose (Old English).

**Chahel** good cheer (Indian).

**Chaim** a variant form of *Hyam*.

**Chandler** a surname, meaning maker or seller of candles, used as a first name (Old French).

**Chandran** moon (Indian).

**Chapman** a surname, meaning merchant, used as a first name (Old English).

**Charles** strong; manly; noble-spirited (Germanic); a diminutive form is *Charlie*.

**Chase** a surname, meaning hunter, used as a first name (Old French).

**Chester** a placename, meaning Roman fortified camp, used as a first name (Old English).

**Chinmayu** supreme consciousness (Indian).

**Chintan** a thought (Indian).

**Chirag** lamp (Indian).

**Chiranjiv** immortal (Indian).

**Cholan** a South Indian dynasty (Hindu).

**Christian** belonging to Christ; a believer in Christ (Latin); diminutive forms are *Chris, Christie, Christy*.

**Christmas** festival of Christ (Old English).

**Christopher** bearing Christ (Greek); diminutive forms are *Chris, Christie, Christy, Kester, Kit*.

**Churchill** a placename and

surname, meaning church on a hill, used as a first name (Old English).

**Cian** ancient (Irish Gaelic); anglicized forms are *Kean, Keane*.

**Ciarán** small and black (Irish Gaelic); the anglicized form is *Kieran*.

**Clarence** bright, shining (Latin); a diminutive form is *Clarrie*.

**Clark, Clarke** a surname, meaning cleric, scholar or clerk, used as a first name (Old French).

**Claudius** lame (Latin); the Dutch and German forms of *Claud*.

**Claus** a variant form of *Klaus*.

**Clayborne** a surname, meaning a dweller in a place with clay soil by a brook, used as a first name (Old English); a variant form is *Claiborne*; a diminutive form is *Clay*.

**Clayton** a placename and surname, meaning place in or with good clay, used as a first name (Old English); a diminutive form is *Clay*.

**Clement** mild-tempered, merciful (Latin); a diminutive form is *Clem*.

**Cleveland** a placename, meaning land of hills, used as a first name (Old English).

**Clifford** a surname, meaning ford at a cliff, used as a first name (Old English); a diminutive form is *Cliff*.

**Clifton** a placename, meaning place on a cliff, used as a first name (Old English).

**Clinton** a placename and surname, meaning settlement on a hill, used as a first name; a diminutive form is *Clint*.

**Clive** a surname, meaning at the cliff, used as a first name (Old English).

**Clovis** warrior (Germanic).

**Clyde** the name of a Scottish river, meaning cleansing one, used as a first name.

**Cody** a surname used as a first name.

**Colby** from the dark country (Norse).

**Coleman** a surname, meaning swarthy man or servant of Nicholas, used as a first name (Old English).

**Colin** a diminutive form of *Nicholas*, long used independently.

**Collier, Collyer** a surname, meaning charcoal seller or burner, used as a first name (Old English); a variant form is *Colyer*.

**Colm** dove (Irish Gaelic/Latin).

**Colman, Colmán** keeper of doves (Irish Gaelic/Latin); diminutive forms are *Col, Cole*.

**Columba** dove (Latin); a diminutive form is *Coly*.

**Comyn** bent (Irish Gaelic).

**Conan, Cónán** little hound (Irish Gaelic); a diminutive form is *Con*.

**Conn** chief (Celtic).

**Connall** courageous (Irish and Scots Gaelic).

**Connor** high desire or will (Irish Gaelic).

**Conrad** able counsellor (Germanic); a diminutive form is *Con*.

**Conroy** wise (Gaelic).

**Constant** firm; faithful (Latin); a diminutive form is *Con*.

**Constantine** resolute; firm (Latin).

**Conway** a surname, of uncertain meaning – possibly yellow hound or head-smashing, used as a first name (Irish Gaelic); high or holy water (Welsh).

**Cooper** a surname, meaning barrel maker, used as a first name (Old English); a diminutive form is *Coop*.

**Corbet, Corbett** a surname, meaning raven, black-haired or raucousness, used as a first name (Old French).

**Corcoran** a surname, meaning red- or purple-faced, used as a first name (Irish Gaelic).

**Corey** a surname, meaning good peace, used as a first name (Irish Gaelic).

**Cormac, Cormack, Cormick** charioteer (Irish Gaelic).

**Cornelius** origin uncertain, possibly horn-like, a Roman family name; a variant form is *Cornell*.

**Corwin** friend of the heart (Old French).

**Cosimo** an Italian form of *Cosmo*.

**Cosmo** order, beauty (Greek).

**Courtney** a surname, meaning short nose, used as a first name (Old French).

**Craig** a surname meaning crag, used as a first name (Scots Gaelic).

**Cranley** a surname, meaning crane clearing, spring or meadow, used as a first name (Old English).

**Crawford** a placename and surname, meaning ford of the crows, used as a first name (Old English).

**Creighton** a surname, meaning rock or cliff place (Old Welsh/Old English) or border settlement (Scots Gaelic), used as a first name (Old English).

**Crispin, Crispian** having curly hair (Latin).

**Crosbie, Crosby** a placename and surname, meaning farm or village with crosses, used as a first name (Old Norse).

**Cullan, Cullen** a surname,

meaning Cologne, used as a first name (Old French); a placename, meaning at the back of the river, used as a first name (Scots Gaelic).

**Curran** a surname, of uncertain meaning – possibly resolute hero, used as a first name (Irish Gaelic).

**Curtis** a surname, meaning courteous, educated, used as a first name (Old French); a diminutive form is *Curt*.

**Cuthbert** famous bright (Old English).

**Cyprian** from Cyprus, the Mediterranean island (Greek).

**Cyrano** from Cyrene, an ancient city of North Africa (Greek).

**Cyril** lordly (Greek).

**Cyrus** the sun (Persian); a diminutive form Is *Cy*.

# D

**Dafydd** a Welsh form of *David*.

**Dag** day (Norse).

**Dagan** earth, the name of an earth god of the Assyrians and Babylonians (Semitic).

**Dai** a Welsh diminutive form of *David*, formerly a name in its own right, meaning shining.

**Dakshi** the glorious (Indian).

**Dale** a surname, meaning valley, used as a first name (Old English).

**Daley** a surname, meaning assembly, used as a first name (Irish Gaelic); a variant form is *Daly*.

**Dallas** a surname, meaning meadow resting place (Scots Gaelic) or dale house (Old English), used as a first name.

**Dalton** a surname, meaning dale farm, used as a first name (Old English).

**Dalziel** a placename and surname, meaning field of the sungleam, used as a first name (Scots Gaelic).

**Damien** taming (Greek).

**Damon** conqueror (Greek).

**Dane** a surname, meaning valley, used as a first name (Old English).

**Daniel** God is my judge (Hebrew); diminutive forms are *Dan, Dannie, Danny*.

**Dante** steadfast (Latin/Italian).

**Danvir** charitable (Indian).

**Darcy, D'Arcy** a surname, meaning fortress, used as a first name (Old French).

**Darien** a South American placename also used as a first name.

**Darius** preserver (Persian).

**Darnell** a surname, meaning hidden nook, used as a first name (Old English).

**Darrell, Darrel** from a surname, meaning from Airelle in Normandy, used as a first name; variant forms are *Darell, Darryl, Daryl*.

**Darren, Darin** a surname, of unknown origin, used as a first name.

**Darton** a surname, meaning deer enclosure or forest, used as a first name (Old English).

**Dattatreya** a son of Atri, a god (Hindu).

**David** beloved (Hebrew); diminutive forms are *Dave, Davie, Davy*.

**Davis** David's son (Old English).

**Dayaram** merciful (Indian).

**Dean** a surname, meaning one who lives in a valley (Old English) or serving as a dean (Old French), used as a first name; the anglicized form of *Dino*.

**Dearborn** a surname, meaning deer brook, used as a first name (Old English).

**Decimus** tenth (Latin).

**Declan** the name, of unknown meaning, of a 5th-century Irish saint (Irish Gaelic).

**Dedrick** people's ruler (Germanic).

**Deepak** lamp (Indian).

**Deinol** charming (Welsh).

**Dell** a surname, meaning one who lives in a hollow, used as a first name; a diminutive form of *Delmar*, etc.

**Delmar** of the sea (Latin).

**Delwyn, Delwin** neat and blessed (Welsh).

**Demetrius** belonging to Demeter, goddess of the harvest, earth mother (Greek).

**Dempsey** a surname, meaning proud descendant, used as a first name (Gaelic).

**Dempster** a surname, meaning judge, used as a first name, formerly a feminine one (Old English).

**Denis, Dennis** belonging to Dionysus, the god of wine (Greek).

**Denman** a surname, meaning dweller in a valley, used as a first name (Old English).

**Dennison** son of Dennis (Old English); variant forms are *Denison, Tennison, Tennyson*.

**Denton** a surname, meaning valley place, used as a first name (Old English).

**Denver** a surname, meaning Danes' crossing, used as a first name (Old English).

**Denzel, Denzell, Denzil** a surname, meaning stronghold, used as a first name (Celtic).

**Derek** an English form of Theoderic; variant forms are

*Derrick, Derrik*; a diminutive form is *Derry*.

**Derwent** a placename and surname, meaning river that flows through oak woods, used as a first name (Old English).

**Desmond** a variant form of Esmond (Germanic).

**Dev** divinity (Indian).

**Devarsi** sage of the Devas (Hindu).

**Deverell, Deverill** a surname, meaning fertile river bank, used as a first name (Celtic).

**Devin, Devinn** a surname, meaning poet, used as a first name (Irish Gaelic); a variant form is *Davin*.

**Devlin** fiercely brave (Irish Gaelic).

**Devrat** spiritual (Indian).

**Devon** the name of the English county, meaning deep ones, used as a first name (Celtic).

**Dewey** a Celtic form of David.

**Dewi** a Welsh form of David.

**Dexter** a surname, meaning (woman) dyer, used as a first name (Old English).

**Dhairya** patience (Indian).

**Dharuna** a rishi (Hindu).

**Dhiraj** patience (Indian).

**Dhruv** firm (Indian).

**Diarmaid** free of envy (Irish Gaelic); a variant form is *Diarmuid*; the anglicized form is *Dermot*.

**Dickson** a surname, meaning son of Richard, used as a first name (Old English); a variant form is *Dixon*.

**Diego** a Spanish form of James.

**Dietrich** the German form of Derek.

**Digby** a surname, meaning settlement at a ditch, used as a first name (Old Norse).

**Dilip** a king, ancestor of Rama (Hindu).

**Dillon** a surname of uncertain meaning, possibly destroyer, used as a first name (Germanic/Irish Gaelic).

**Dinesh** sun (Indian).

**Dino** a diminutive ending, indicating little, now used independently (Italian).

**Dion** a shortened form of Dionysus, the god of wine (Greek); a variant form is *Deon*.

**Dipendu** moon (Indian).

**Dirk** the Dutch form of Derek; a diminutive form of Theodoric.

**Diyaa Udeen** brightness of the faith (Indian).

**Dolan** a variant form of Doolan.

**Dominic, Dominick** belonging to the lord (Latin); a diminutive form is *Dom*.

**Donal** anglicized forms of Dónal; a variant form is *Donall*; diminutive forms are *Don, Donnie, Donny*.

**Donald** proud chief (Scots

Gaelic); diminutive forms are *Don, Donnie, Donny*.

**Donato** gift of God (Latin).

**Doran** a surname, meaning stranger or exile, used as a first name (Irish Gaelic).

**Dorian** man, one of a Hellenic people who invaded Greece in the 2nd century BC (Greek); its use as a first name was probably invented by Oscar Wilde for his novel, *The Portrait of Dorian Gray*.

**Dougal, Dougall** black stranger (Gaelic); variant forms are *Dugal, Dugald*; diminutive forms are *Doug, Dougie, Duggie*.

**Douglas** a placename, meaning black water, used as a first name (Scots Gaelic); diminutive forms are *Doug, Dougie, Duggie*.

**Dow** a surname, meaning black or black-haired, used as a first name (Scots Gaelic).

**Doyle** an Irish Gaelic form of Dougal.

**Drake** a surname, meaning dragon or standard bearer, used as a first name (Old English).

**Drew** a diminutive form of Andrew; a surname, meaning trusty (Germanic) or lover (Old French) used as a first name.

**Driscoll, Driscol** a surname, meaning interpreter, used as a first name (Irish Gaelic).

**Druce** a surname meaning from Eure or Rieux in France (Old French), or a sturdy lover, used as a first name (Celtic).

**Drummond** a surname, meaning ridge, used as a first name.

**Drury** a surname, meaning dear one, used as a first name (Old French).

**Dryden** a surname, meaning dry valley, used as a first name (Old English).

**Duane** dark (Irish Gaelic); variant forms are *Dwane, Dwayne*.

**Dudley** a placename, meaning Dudda's clearing, used as a first name (Old English).

**Duke** the title of an English aristocrat used as a first name; a diminutive form of Marmaduke.

**Dulal** loved one (Indian).

**Duncan** brown chief (Gaelic); a diminutive form is *Dunc*.

**Dunlop** a surname, meaning muddy hill, used as a first name (Scots Gaelic).

**Dunn, Dunne** a surname, meaning dark-skinned, used as a first name (Old English).

**Dunstan** brown hill stone (Old English).

**Durand, Durant** a surname, meaning enduring or obstinate, used as a first name (Old French).

**Duranjaya** a heroic son (Hindu).

**Durijesh** moon (Indian).

**Durjaya** difficult to conquer (Hindu).

**Durward** a surname, meaning doorkeeper or gatekeeper, used as a first name (Old English); a variant form is *Dorward*.

**Durwin** dear friend (Old English); a diminutive form is *Durwyn*.

**Dushyant** destroyer of evil (Indian).

**Dustin** a surname, of uncertain meaning – possibly of Dionysus, used as a first name.

**Dwight** a surname, meaning Thor's stone, used as a first name (Old Norse).

**Dyfan** ruler (Welsh).

**Dylan** sea (Welsh).

# E

**Eachan, Eachann, Eacheann** horse (Scots Gaelic).

**Eamon, Eamonn** an Irish Gaelic form of Edmund.

**Earl, Earle** an English title, meaning nobleman, used as a first name (Old English); a variant form is *Erle*.

**Eaton** a surname, meaning river or island farm, used as a first name (Old English).

**Eben** stone (Hebrew); a diminutive form is *Eb*.

**Ebenezer** stone of help (Hebrew); diminutive forms are *Eb, Eben*.

**Edan** a Scottish form of Aidan.

**Edbert** prosperous; bright (Old English).

**Edelmar** noble, famous (Old English).

**Eden** pleasantness (Hebrew); a surname, meaning blessed helmet, sometimes used as a first name.

**Edgar** prosperity spear (Old English); diminutive forms are *Ed, Eddie, Eddy, Ned, Neddie, Neddy*.

**Edi** herb (Indian).

**Edmond** the French form of Edmund.

**Edmund** prosperity defender (Old English).

**Ednit** evolved (Indian).

**Edric** wealthy ruler (Old English).

**Edryd** restoration (Welsh).

**Edsel** noble (Germanic).

**Edwald** prosperous ruler (Old English).

**Edward** guardian of happiness (Old English); diminutive forms are *Ed, Eddie, Eddy, Ned, Ted, Teddy*.

**Edwin** prosperity friend (Old English).

**Eeshwar** god (Indian).

**Egan** a surname, meaning son of Hugh, used as a first name (Irish Gaelic).

**Egbert** sword bright (Germanic).

**Egidio** the Italian and Spanish form of Giles.

**Ehimay** all pervasive (Indian).

**Eha** Lord Vishnu (Indian).

**Ehren** honourable one (Germanic).

**Eilir** butterfly (Welsh).

**Einar** single warrior (Old Norse).

**Ekagrah** focused (Indian).

**Ekaraj** emperor (Indian).

**Ekavir** bravest of the brave (Indian).

**Ekbal** dignity (Indian).

**Elder** a surname, meaning senior, elder, used as a first name (Old English).

**Eldon** a surname, meaning Ella's hill, used as a first name (Old English).

**Eldred** terrible (Old English).

**Eldrid, Eldridge** wise adviser (Old English).

**Elfed** autumn (Welsh).

**Elgan** bright circle (Welsh).

**Elias** a variant form of Elijah; a diminutive form is *Eli*.

**Elihu** he is my God (Hebrew).

**Elijah** Jehovah is my God (Hebrew); a diminutive form is *Lije*.

**Eliot** a variant form of Elliot.

**Elisha** God is salvation (Hebrew).

**Elliot, Elliot** a surname, from a French diminutive form of Elias, used as a first name.

**Ellis** a surname, a Middle English form of Elias, used as a first name.

**Ellison** a surname, meaning son of Elias, used as a first name (Old English).

**Elmer** noble; excellent (Germanic).

**Elmo** amiable (Greek).

**Elmore** a surname, meaning river bank with elms, used as a first name (Old English).

**Elroy** a variant form of Leroy.

**Elton** a surname, meaning settlement of Ella, used as a first name (Old English).

**Elvey** a surname, meaning elf gift, used as a first name (Old English); a variant form is *Elvy*.

**Elvin** a surname, meaning elf or noble friend, used as a first name (Old English); a variant form is *Elwin*.

**Elvis** wise one (Norse).

**Elwin** a variant form of Elvin; white brow (Welsh); a variant form is *Elwyn*.

**Emil** of a noble Roman family the origin of whose name, Aemilius, is uncertain.

**Emlyn** origin uncertain, possibly from Emil (Welsh).

**Emmanuel** God with us (Hebrew); a variant form is *Immanuel*; a diminutive form is *Manny*.

**Emmett** industrious (Germanic/Old English).

**Emory** a variant form of Amory.

**Emrys** a Welsh form of Ambrose.

**Engelbert** bright angel (Germanic).

**Ennis** chief one (Gaelic).

**Enoch** dedication (Hebrew).

**Enos** man (Hebrew).

**Enrico** the Italian form of Henry.

**Eoin** an Irish form of John.

**Ephraim** fruitful (Hebrew); a diminutive form is *Eph*.

**Erasmus** lovely; worthy of love (Greek); a diminutive form is *Ras, Rasmus*.

**Erastus** beloved (Greek); diminutive forms are *Ras, Rastus*.

**Eric** rich; brave; powerful (Old English); a variant form is *Erik*.

**Erland** stranger (Old Norse).

**Ernest** earnestness (Germanic); diminutive forms are *Ern, Ernie*.

**Erskine** a placename and surname, meaning projecting height, used as a first name (Scots Gaelic).

**Eryl** watcher (Welsh).

**Esau** hairy (Hebrew).

**Esmé** beloved (French).

**Esmond** divine protection (Old English).

**Este** man from the East (Italian).

**Estéban** the Spanish form of Stephen.

**Etash** luminous (Indian).

**Ethan** firm (Hebrew).

**Etienne** the French form of Stephen.

**Ettore** the Italian form of Hector.

**Eugene** well-born; noble (Greek); a diminutive form is *Gene*.

**Eurig, Euros** gold (Welsh).

**Eusebio** pious (Greek).

**Eustace** rich (Greek); diminutive forms are *Stacey, Stacy*.

**Evan** young warrior (Celtic).

**Evelyn** the English surname used as a first name.

**Everley** field of the wild boar (Old English).

**Evyavan** Lord Vishnu (Indian).

**Ewan, Ewen** Irish and Scots Gaelic forms of Owen; a Scottish form of Eugene; a variant form is *Euan*.

**Ewart** an Old French variant of Edward; a surname, meaning herd of ewes used as a first name (Old English).

**Ezekiel** strength of God (Hebrew); a diminutive form is *Zeke*.

**Ezra** help (Hebrew).

# F

**Faaris** horseman (Indian).
**Faarooq** he who distinguishes truth from falsehood (Indian).
**Faber, Fabre** a surname, meaning smith, used as a first name (Latin).
**Fabian** the anglicized form of the Roman family name Fabianus, derived from Fabius, from faba, bean (Latin).
**Fadi** redeemer (Indian).
**Fahad** lynx (Indian).
**Fairfax** the surname, meaning lovely hair, used as a first name (Old English).
**Fairley, Fairlie** a surname, meaning clearing with ferns, used as a first name (Old English).
**Faisal** decisive (Indian).
**Fane** a surname, meaning glad or eager, used as a first name (Old English).
**Farnall, Farnell** a surname, meaning fern hill, used as a first name (Old English); variant forms are *Fernald, Fernall*.
**Farquhar** friendly man (Scots Gaelic).
**Farr** a surname, meaning bull, used as a first name (Old English).

**Farrell** warrior (Irish Gaelic).
**Fateen** clever (Indian).
**Fawaz** successful (Indian).
**Felix** happy (Latin).
**Felton** a placename and surname, meaning place in a field, used as a first name (Old English).
**Fenton** a placename and surname, meaning a place in marshland or fens, used as a first name (Old English).
**Ferdinand** peace (Germanic); diminutive forms are *Ferd, Ferdy*.
**Fergal** man of strength (Irish Gaelic); diminutive forms are *Fergie, Fergy*.
**Fergus** vigorous man (Irish/Scots Gaelic); diminutive forms are *Fergie, Fergy*.
**Ferguson, Fergusson** a surname, meaning son of Fergus, used as a first name; diminutive forms are *Fergie, Fergy*.
**Fernald, Fernall** variant forms of Farnall, Farnell.
**Fidaa** redemption (Indian).
**Fidelis** faithful (Latin); a diminutive form is *Fid*.
**Fielding** a surname, meaning dweller in a field, used as a first name (Old English).
**Fingal** white stranger (Scots Gaelic).
**Finlay, Finley** fair warrior or

calf (Scots Gaelic); a variant form is *Findlay*.

**Finn** fair, white (Irish Gaelic); a variant form is *Fionn*.

**Fitz** son (Old French); a diminutive form of names beginning with Fitz.

**Fitzgerald** a surname, meaning son of Gerald, used as a first name (Old French).

**Fitzhugh** a surname, meaning son of Hugh, used as a first name (Old French).

**Fitzpatrick** a surname, meaning son of Patrick, used as a first name (Old French).

**Fitzroy** a surname, meaning (illegitimate) son of the king, used as a first name (Old French).

**Flann** red-haired (Irish Gaelic).

**Flannan** red-complexioned (Irish Gaelic).

**Flavian, Flavius** masculine forms of Flavia.

**Fleming** a surname, meaning man from Flanders, used as a first name (Old French).

**Fletcher** a surname meaning arrow-maker, used as a first name (Old French).

**Flint** stream, brook (Old English).

**Florian** flowering, blooming (Latin).

**Floyd** a variant form of the surname Lloyd used as a first name.

**Flynn** a surname, meaning son of the red-haired one, used as a first name (Scots Gaelic); a variant form is *Flinn*.

**Forbes** a placename and surname, meaning fields or district, used as a first name (Scots Gaelic).

**Ford** the English word for a crossing place of a river used as a first name (Old English).

**Forrest** a surname, meaning forest, used as a first name (Old French).

**Forrester, Forster** a surname, meaning forester, used as a first name (Old French).

**Foster** a surname, meaning forester or cutler (Old French) or foster parent (Old English), used as a first name.

**Francesco** the Italian form of Francis; a contracted form is *Franco*.

**Francis** free (Germanic); diminutive forms are *Fra, Frank, Francie*.

**François** the French form of Francis.

**Frank** Frenchman (Old French) a diminutive form of Francis, Franklin; diminutive forms are *Frankie, Franky*.

**Franklin, Franklen, Franklyn** a surname, meaning freeholder, used as a first name (Old French); diminutive forms are

Frank, Frankie, Franky.

**Fraser, Frasier** a Scottish surname, meaning from Frisselle or Fresel in France; variant forms are *Frazer, Frazier*.

**Frayn, Frayne** a surname, meaning ash tree, used as a surname (Old French); a variant form is *Fraine*.

**Frederick, Frederic** abounding in peace; peaceful ruler (Germanic); diminutive forms are *Fred, Freddie, Freddy*.

**Freeman** a surname, meaning free man, used as first name (Old English).

**Frewin** a surname, meaning generous friend, used as a first name (Old English).

**Fuad** heart (Indian).

**Fulton** a surname, meaning muddy place, used as a first name (Old English).

**Fyfe, Fyffe** a surname, meaning from Fife, used as a first name.

# G

**Gabriel** strength of God; man of God; in the Bible one of the archangels (Hebrew); a diminutive form is *Gabe*.

**Gad** good luck, good fortune (Hebrew).

**Gagan** sky (Indian).

**Gajendra** elephant king (Hindu).

**Galen** the anglicized form of the Roman family name Galenus, calmer (Latin).

**Gallagher** a surname, meaning foreign helper, used as a first name (Irish Gaelic).

**Galloway** a placename and surname, meaning stranger.

**Gaels**, used as a first name (Old Welsh).

**Galton** a surname, meaning rented farm, used as a first name (Old English).

**Galvin** bright, white (Irish Gaelic).

**Gamaliel** recompense of God (Hebrew).

**Gandhi** sun (Indian).

**Gandhik** fragrance (Indian).

**Gareth** old man (Welsh); diminutive forms are *Gary, Garry*; a variant form is *Garth*.

**Garfield** a surname, meaning triangular piece of open land, used as a first name (Old English).

**Garnet, Garnett** a surname, meaning pomegranate, used as a first name (Old French).

**Garret, Garrett** the Irish Gaelic form of Gerard; a variant form of Garrard.

**Garrison** a surname, meaning son of Garret, used as a first name (Old English).

**Garth** a surname, meaning garden or paddock, used as a first name (Old Norse); a variant form of Gareth.

**Garton** a surname, meaning fenced farm, used as a first name (Old Norse).

**Garve** a placename, meaning rough place, used as a first name (Scots Gaelic).

**Gary** spear carrier (Germanic); a diminutive form of Gareth; a variant form is *Garry*.

**Gaston** stranger, guest (Germanic); from Gascony (Old French).

**Gaurav** prestige (Indian).

**Gavin** an anglicized form of Gawain.

**Gawain** white hawk (Welsh).

**Gaylord** a surname, meaning brisk noble man, used as a first name (Old French).

**Gene** a diminutive form of Eugene, now used independently.

**Geoffrey** a variant form of Jeffrey; a diminutive form is *Geoff*.

**George** a landholder; husbandman (Germanic); diminutive forms are *Geordie, Georgie, Georgy*.

**Geraint** old man (Welsh).

**Gerald** strong with the spear (Germanic); diminutive forms are *Gerrie, Gerry, Jerry*.

**Gerard** firm spear (Old German); variant forms are *Garrard, Garratt, Gerrard*; diminutive forms are *Gerrie, Gerry, Jerry*.

**Germain** brother (Latin).

**Gervase** spearman (Germanic); variant forms are *Gervaise, Jarvis, Jervis*.

**Gethin** dusky (Welsh).

**Giacomo** an Italian form of James.

**Gibson** a surname, meaning son of Gilbert, used as a first name (Old English).

**Gideon** a destroyer (Hebrew).

**Giffard, Gifford** a surname, meaning bloated (Old French) or gift (Germanic), used as a first name.

**Gilbert** yellow-bright; famous (Germanic); diminutive form is *Gil*.

**Gilchrist** servant of Christ (Scots Gaelic); a diminutive form is *Gil*.

**Giles** a kid (Greek); a diminutive form is *Gil*.

**Gilles** the French form of Giles.

**Gillespie** a surname, meaning servant of a bishop, used as a first name (Scots Gaelic).

**Gilmore, Gilmour** a surname, meaning servant of St Mary, used as a first name (Scots Gaelic); a variant form is *Gillmore*.

**Gilroy** a surname, meaning servant of the red-haired one, used as a first name (Gaelic).

**Giorgio** the Italian form of George.

**Giovanni** the Italian form of John; diminutive forms are *Gian, Gianni.*

**Girvan** a placename, meaning short river, used as a first name (Scots Gaelic).

**Giuseppe** the Italian form of Joseph; a diminutive form is *Beppe, Beppo.*

**Gladwin** a surname, meaning glad friend, used as a first name (Old English).

**Glanville** dweller on the oak tree estate (French); a diminutive form is *Glanvil.*

**Glen** the surname, meaning a valley, used as a first name (Scots Gaelic); a variant form is *Glenn.*

**Glendon** from the fortress in the Glen (Celtic).

**Glyn** valley (Welsh); a variant form is *Glynn.*

**Goddard** pious; virtuous (Old German).

**Godfrey** at peace with God (Germanic).

**Godwin** God's friend (Old English).

**Golding** a surname, meaning son of gold, used as a first name (Old English).

**Goldwin** golden friend (Old English).

**Goliath** mighty warrior (Hebrew).

**Goodwin** a surname, meaning good friend, used as a first name (Old English).

**Gordon** a surname, meaning great hill, used as a first name (Scots Gaelic).

**Grady** a surname, meaning noble, used as a first name (Irish Gaelic).

**Graham, Grahame, Graeme** a Scottish surname, 'meaning one who lives by the grey land', used as a first name (Celtic).

**Granger** a surname, meaning farmer or bailiff, used as a first name (Old English).

**Grant** a surname, meaning large, used as a first name (Norman French).

**Granville** large town (Old French).

**Gray** a surname, meaning grey-haired, used as a first name (Old English); a variant form is *Grey.*

**Greeley** a surname, meaning pitted, used as a first name (Old English).

**Gregor** a Scots form of Gregory.

**Gregory** watchful (Greek); a diminutive form is *Greg.*

**Gresham** a surname, meaning grazing meadow, used as a first name (Old English).

**Greville** a surname, meaning from Gréville in France, used as a first name.

**Grier** a surname, a contracted form of Gregor.

**Griffin** a Latinized form of Griffith; a diminutive form is *Griff*.

**Griffith** an anglicized form of Gruffydd; a diminutive form is *Griff*.

**Grishm** heat (Indian).

**Grover** a surname, meaning from a grove of trees, used as a first name (Old English).

**Gruffydd** powerful chief (Welsh).

**Guido** the German, Italian and Spanish forms of Guy.

**Guilbert** a French form of Gilbert.

**Guillaume** the French form of William.

**Gunnar** the Scandinavian form of Gunter.

**Gunter** battle warrior (Germanic).

**Gustave** staff of the Goths (Swedish); a diminutive form is *Gus*.

**Guthrie** a surname, meaning windy, used as a first name (Scots Gaelic).

**Guy** a leader (German-French).

**Gwyn, Gwynn** fair, blessed (Welsh); diminutive forms are *Gwyn, Guin*.

**Gwynfor** fair lord (Welsh).

# H

**Haddan, Hadden, Haddon** a surname, meaning heathery hill, used as a first name (Old English).

**Hadley** a surname, meaning heathery hill or heathery meadow, used as a first name (Old English).

**Hadrian** a variant form of Adrian.

**Hagan, Hagan** young Hugh (Irish Gaelic); thorn bush or thorn fence (Germanic).

**Hagley** a surname, meaning haw wood or clearing, used as a first name (Old English).

**Haig** a first name, meaning one who lives in an enclosure, used as a first name (Old English).

**Hakon** from the exalted race (Old Norse); a variant form is *Haakon*; a diminutive form is *Hako*.

**Halbert** brilliant hero (Old English); a diminutive form is *Hal*.

**Hale** a surname, meaning from the hall, used as a surname (Old English).

**Halford** a surname, meaning from a ford in a hollow, used as a first name (Old English).

**Hall** a surname, meaning one who lives at a manor house, used as a first name (Old English).

**Hallam** a surname, meaning at the hollow (Old English), or a placename, meaning at the rocky place (Old Norse), used as a first name.

**Halliwell** a surname, meaning one who lives by the holy well, used as a first name (Old English); a variant form is *Haliwell*.

**Halstead, Halsted** a surname, meaning from the stronghold, used as a first name (Old English).

**Halton** a surname, meaning from the lookout hill, used as a first name (Old English).

**Hamar** strong man (Old Norse).

**Hamilton** a surname, meaning farm in broken country, used as a first name (Old English).

**Hamish** a Scots Gaelic form of James.

**Hammad** one who praises God (Indian).

**Hammonda** surname, meaning belonging to Hamon, used as a first name (Old English).

**Hamon** great protection (Old English).

**Hamza** lion (Indian).

**Hanford** a surname, meaning rocky ford or ford with cocks, used as a first name (Old English).

**Hanley** a surname, meaning from the high meadow or hill, used as a first name (Old English).

**Hannibal** grace of Baal (Punic).

**Hans** a diminutive form of Johann.

**Hansel** gift from God (Scandinavian).

**Harcourt** a surname, meaning from a fortified court (Old French), or falconer's cottage (Old English), used as a first name.

**Harding** a surname, meaning brave warrior, used as a first name (Old English).

**Hardy** a surname, meaning bold and daring, used as a first name (Germanic); variant forms are *Hardey, Hardie*.

**Harford** a surname, meaning stags' ford, used as a first name (Old English).

**Hargrave, Hargreave, Hargreaves** a surname, meaning from the hare grove, used as a first name (Old English).

**Harij** the horizon (Indian).

**Harindra** a tree (Indian).

**Harlan, Harland** a surname, meaning rocky land, used as a first name (Old English).

**Harley** a surname, meaning from the hare meadow or hill, used as a first name (Old English).

**Harlow** a placename and surname, meaning fortified hill, used as a first name (Old English).

**Harold** a champion; general of an army (Old English).

**Harper** a surname, meaning harp player or maker, used as a first name (Old English).

**Harris, Harrison** surnames, meaning son of Harold or Harry, used as first names (Old English).

**Harry** a diminutive form of Henry, also used independently.

**Hart** a surname, meaning hart deer, used as a first name (Old English).

**Hartford** a placename and surname, meaning ford of the deer, or army ford, used as a first name (Old English); a variant form is *Hertford*.

**Hartley** a surname, meaning clearing with stags, used as a first name (Old English).

**Hartmann, Hartman** strong and brave (Germanic).

**Hartwell** a surname, meaning stags' stream, used as a first name (Old English).

**Harvey, Harvie** a surname, meaning battle worthy, used as a first name (Breton Gaelic); a variant form is *Hervey*.

**Hastings** a placename and surname, meaning territory of the violent ones, used as a first name (Old English).

**Havelock** a surname, meaning sea battle, used as a first name (Old Norse).

**Hawley** a surname, meaning from a hedged meadow, used as a first name (Old English).

**Hayden, Haydon** a surname, meaning heather hill or hay hill, used as a first name (Old English).

**Haytham** young hawk (Indian).

**Hayward** a surname, meaning supervisor of enclosures, used as a first name (Old English); a variant form is *Heyward*.

**Haywood** a surname, meaning fenced forest, used as a first name (Old English); a variant form is *Heywood*.

**Heath** a surname, meaning heathland, used as a first name (Old English).

**Heathcliff, Heathcliffe** dweller by the heather cliff (Old English).

**Hector** holding fast (Greek).

**Heinrich** the German form of Henry; diminutive forms are *Heinz, Heinze*.

**Henry** the head or chief of a house (Germanic); diminutive forms are *Harry, Hal, Hank*.

**Herbert** army bright (Old

English); a variant form is *Harbert*; diminutive forms are *Herb, Herbie*.

**Hercules** glory of Hera (the Latin form of the name of Herakles, the Greek hero, son of Zeus and stepson of Hera).

**Herman** warrior (Germanic).

**Hermes** in Greek mythology, the messenger of the gods, with winged feet. His counterpart in Roman mythology is Mercury.

**Herrick** a surname, meaning powerful army, used as a first name (Old Norse).

**Hesketh** a surname, meaning horse track, used as a first name (Old Norse).

**Hew** a Welsh form of Hugh.

**Hewett, Hewit** a surname, meaning little Hugh or cleared place, used as a first name (Old English).

**Hilary, Hillary** cheerful; merry (Latin).

**Hilton** a surname, meaning from the hill farm, used as a first name (Old English); a variant form is *Hylton*.

**Hiresh** king of precious stones (Indian).

**Hogan** youthful (Irish Gaelic).

**Holbrook** a surname, meaning brook in the valley, used as a first name (Old English).

**Holcomb, Holcombe** a surname, meaning deep valley, used as a first name (Old English).

**Holden** a surname, meaning from the deep valley, used as a first name (Old English).

**Holgate** a surname, meaning road in a hollow, used as a first name (Old English).

**Hollis** a surname, meaning dweller near holly trees, used as a first name (Old English).

**Holmes** a surname, meaning an island in a river, used as a first name (Old English).

**Holt** a surname, meaning a wood or forest, used as a first name (Old English).

**Homer** uncertain, possibly hostage (Greek); the name of the Greek epic poet of the first millennium BC.

**Horace, Horatio** origin uncertain, possibly a family name Horatius (Latin).

**Horton** a surname, meaning muddy place, used as a first name (Old English).

**Houghton** a surname, meaning place in an enclosure, used as a first name (Old English); a variant form is *Hutton*.

**Houston, Houstun** a surname, meaning Hugh's place, used as a first name (Old English).

**Howard** a surname, meaning mind strong, used as a first name (Germanic).

**Howe** a surname, meaning high one (Germanic) or hill (Old English) used as a first name.

**Hubert** mind bright (Germanic); a variant surname form is *Hobart*.

**Hudson** a surname, meaning son of little Hugh, used as a first name (Old English).

**Hugh** mind; spirit (Germanic).

**Hugo** the Latin, German and Spanish form of Hugh.

**Hulbert, Hulburd, Hulburt** a surname, meaning brilliant, gracious, used as a first name (Germanic); variant forms are *Holbert, Holbird*.

**Humbert** bright warrior (Germanic).

**Humphrey, Humphry** giant peace (Old English).

**Hunt, Hunter** surnames, meaning hunter, used as first names (Old English).

**Huntingdon** a placename and surname, meaning hunter's hill, used as a first name (Old English).

**Huntington** a surname, meaning hunter's farm, used as a first name (Old English).

**Huntley, Huntly** a surname, meaning hunter's meadow, used as a first name (Old English).

**Hurley** sea tide (Gaelic).

**Hurst** a surname, meaning wooded hill, used as a first name (Old English).

**Hussein** beautiful (Indian).

**Hutton** a variant form of Houghton.

**Huxley** a surname, meaning Hugh's meadow, used as a first name (Old English).

**Hyam** man of life (Hebrew).

**Hyde** a surname, meaning a hide (measurement unit) of land, used as a first name (Old English).

**Hywel, Hywell** sound; whole (Welsh); anglicized forms are *Howel, Howell*.

**I**

**Iain** the Scots Gaelic form of John.

**Igor** the Russian form of Ivor.

**Ike** a diminutive form of Isaac.

**Ingram** a surname, meaning raven angel (Germanic) or river meadow (Old English), used as a first name.

**Inigo** a Spanish form of Ignatius, now used as an English-language form.

**Innes, Inness** a surname, meaning island, used as a first name (Scots Gaelic).

**Iorwerth** handsome nobleman (Welsh); diminutive forms are *Iolo, Iolyn*.

**Irvine, Irving** a surname, meaning fresh or green river, used as a first name (Celtic).

**Irwin** a surname, meaning friend of boars, used as a first name (Old English).

**Isaac** laughter (Hebrew); a variant form is *Izaak*; a diminutive form is *Ike*.

**Isaam** safeguard (Indian).

**Isaiah** salvation of Jehovah (Hebrew).

**Ishaaq** a Prophet's name (Indian).

**Isham** a surname, meaning home on the water, used as a first name (Old English).

**Ishan** the lord of wealth (Indian).

**Ishayu** full of strength (Indian).

**Isidore** gift of Isis (Greek).

**Ismaael** a Prophet's name (Indian).

**Israel** a soldier of God ruling with the Lord (Hebrew).

**Ivan** the Russian form of John.

**Ives** a surname, meaning son of Ive (yew), used as a first name (Germanic).

**Ivor** yew army (Old Norse).

**Iwan** a variant form of Ieuan.

**Izz Udeen** might of the Faith (Indian).

# J

**Jack** a diminutive form of John, now used independently; diminutive forms are *Jackie, Jacky*.

**Jackson** a surname, meaning son of Jack, used as a first name.

**Jacob** supplanter (Hebrew); a diminutive form is *Jake*.

**Jake** a diminutive form of Jacob, now used independently.

**Jamal** beauty (Arabic).

**James** a Christian form of Jacob; diminutive forms are *Jamie, Jim, Jimmy*.

**Jan** a diminutive form of John; the Dutch form of John.

**Jason** healer (Greek); in Greek mythology, the hero who led the Argonauts.

**Jasper** treasure master (Persian).

**Javan** clay (Hebrew).

**Javier** a Portuguese and Spanish form of Xavier.

**Jay** a surname, meaning jay, the bird, used as a first name (Old French); a variant form is *Jaye*; a diminutive form for names beginning with j.

**Jayin** conqueror (Indian).

**Jefferson** a surname, meaning son of Jeffrey or Geoffrey, used as a first name (Old English).

**Jehudi** Jewish (Hebrew); a variant form is *Yehudi*.

**Jeremy, Jeremiah** Jehovah has appointed (Hebrew); a diminutive form is *Jerry*.

**Jerome** holy name (Greek); a diminutive form is *Jerry*.

**Jethro** superiority (Hebrew).

**Job** one persecuted (Hebrew).

**Jocelyn, Jocelin** little Goth (Germanic); diminutive forms are *Jos, Joss*.

**Joel** Jehovah is God (Hebrew).

**Johan** a Swedish form of John.

**John** Jehovah has been gracious (Hebrew); diminutive forms are *Jack, Jackie, Jan, Jock, Johnnie, Johnny*.

**Jonah, Jonas** dove (Hebrew).

**Jonathan, Jonathon** Jehovah gave (Hebrew); a diminutive form is *Jon*.

**Jordan** flowing down (Hebrew).

**Joseph** God shall add (Hebrew); diminutive forms are *Jo, Joe, Joey, Jos*.

**Joshua** Jehovah is salvation (Hebrew); a diminutive form is *Josh*.

**Juan** the Spanish form of John, now used as an English-language form.

**Judah** confession (Hebrew); a diminutive form is *Jude*.

**Julian** sprung from or belonging to Julius (Latin); a variant form is *Jolyon*.

**Julius** downy-bearded (Greek).

**Justin** the English form of Justinus, a Roman family name from Justus (Latin); a variant form is *Justinian*.

# K

**Kamal** lotus flower (Hindu).

**Kane** a surname, meaning warrior, used as a first name (Irish Gaelic).

**Karel** the Czech and Dutch form of Charles.

**Karl** a German form of Charles.

**Kashyap** a sage and friend of Pandavas (Indian).

**Kasimir** peace (Polish).

**Kean, Keane** anglicized forms of *Cian*.

**Kedar** powerful (Arabic).

**Keefe** noble, admirable (Irish Gaelic).

**Keegan** a surname, meaning son of Egan, used as a first name (Irish Gaelic).

**Keenan** a surname, meaning little ancient one, used as a first name (Irish Gaelic).

**Keir** a surname, meaning swarthy, used as a first name (Scots Gaelic).

**Keith** a placename and surname, meaning wood, used as a first name (Celtic).

**Keld** a Danish form of Keith.

**Kelsey** a surname, meaning victory, used as a first name (Old English).

**Kelvin** the name of a Scottish river, meaning narrow water, used as a first name (Scots Gaelic).

**Kemp** a surname, meaning warrior (Old English) or athlete (Middle English), used as a first name.

**Kendall, Kendal, Kendell** a surname, meaning valley of the holy river, used as a first name (Celtic/Old English); a diminutive form is *Ken*.

**Kendrick** a surname, meaning hero, used as a first name (Welsh); a variant form is *Kenrick*; a diminutive form is *Ken*.

**Kenelm** royal helmet (Germanic) a diminutive form is *Ken*.

**Kennard** a surname, meaning strong royal, used as a first name (Germanic) a diminutive form is *Ken*.

**Kennedy** a surname, meaning helmeted or ugly head, used as a first name (Gaelic); a diminutive form is *Ken*.

**Kenneth** fire-born; handsome (Gaelic); diminutive forms are *Ken, Kennie, Kenny*.

**Kent** a surname, meaning from the county of Kent (meaning border), used as a first name (Celtic); a diminutive form of Kennet, Kenton.

**Kenyon** white-haired (Gaelic); a surname, meaning mound of Ennion, used as a first name (Welsh).

**Kern** dark one (Gaelic).

**Kerr** a Scottish form of the surname Carr, sometimes used as a first name; a variant form is *Karr*.

**Kevin, Kevan** comely, loved (Irish Gaelic); a diminutive form is *Kev*.

**Khair Udeen** the good of the Faith (Indian).

**Khairy** charitable (Indian).

**Kieran** an anglicized form of Ciaran.

**Kiernan** a variant form of Tiernan.

**Kingsley** a surname, meaning king's meadow, used as a first name (Old English).

**Kingston** a placename and surname, meaning king's farm, used as a first name (Old English).

**Kinsey** a surname, meaning royal victor, used as a first name (Old English).

**Kiran** sun rays (Indian).

**Kirby** a surname, meaning church village or farm, used as a first name (Old Norse).

**Kish** a gift (Hebrew).

**Knight** a surname, meaning bound to serve a feudal lord as a mounted soldier, used as a first name (Old English).

**Kristen** the Danish form of Christian, now also used in English as a girl's name.

**Kristian** a Swedish form of Christian.

**Kurt** a diminutive form of Conrad, now used independently; a variant form is *Curt*.

**Kyle** narrow (Scots Gaelic).

**L**

**Laban** white (Hebrew).

**Labh** gain (Indian).

**Lachlan** from the land of lakes (Scots Gaelic).

**Lakshman** brother of Rama (Hindu).

**Lambert** illustrious with landed possessions (Germanic).

**Lamond, Lamont** a surname, meaning law giver, used as a first name (Old Norse/Scots Gaelic).

**Lane** a surname, meaning narrow road, lane, used as a first name (Old English).

**Langford** a surname, meaning long ford, used as a first name (Old English).

**Langley** a surname, meaning long meadow, used as a first name (Old English).

**Lars** a Scandinavian form of Laurence.

**Larsen, Larson** son of Lars (Scandinavian).

**Laurence** from Laurentium in Italy, place of laurels (Latin); a variant form is *Lawrence*; diminutive forms are *Larry, Laurie*.

**Lawson** a surname, meaning son of Lawrence, used as a first name (Old English).

**Lawton** a surname, meaning from the place on the hill, used as a first name (Old English).

**Lee** a surname, meaning field or meadow, used as a first name (Old English); a variant form is Leigh.

**Leigh** a variant form of Lee.

**Lennox** a placename and surname, meaning abounding in elm trees, used as a first name (Scots Gaelic).

**Leo** lion (Latin); a variant form is *Leon*.

**Leonard** lion strong (Germanic); a variant form is Lennard; diminutive forms are *Len, Lennie, Lenny*.

**Leopold** bold for the people (Germanic).

**Leroy** the king (Old French); a variant form is *Elroy*; diminutive forms are *Lee, Roy*.

**Leslie** a surname, meaning garden by water, used as a first name (Gaelic).

**Lester** a surname, meaning from the Roman site (i.e. the present city of Leicester), used as a first name (Old English).

**Lewis** bold warrior (Germanic); diminutive forms are *Lew, Lewie*.

**Leyland** a surname, meaning fallow or untilled land, used as a first name (Old English); a variant form is *Leland*.

**Liam** the Irish form of William.

**Lincoln** a placename and surname, meaning the place by the pool, used as a first name (Celtic/Latin).

**Lindall, Lindell** a surname, meaning valley of lime trees, used as a first name (Old English).

**Lindley** a placename and surname, meaning lime tree meadow or flax field, used as a first name (Old English); a variant form is *Linley*.

**Lindsay, Lindsey** a surname, meaning island of Lincoln, used as a first name.

**Linford** a surname, meaning from the ford of the lime tree or flax field, used as a first name (Old English).

**Lionel** young lion (Latin); a diminutive form is *Len*.

**Litton** a placename and surname, meaning loud torrent, used as a first name (Old English); a variant form is *Lytton*.

**Llewelyn** lion-like (Welsh).

**Lloyd** a surname, meaning grey, used as a first name (Welsh).

**Locke** a surname, meaning enclosure, stronghold, used as a first name (Old English).

**Logan** a surname, meaning little hollow, used as a first name (Scots Gaelic).

**Lombard** a surname, meaning long beard, used as a first name (Germanic).

**Lorcan, Lorcán** fierce (Irish Gaelic).

**Loring** a surname, meaning man from Lorraine (bold and famous), used as a first name (Germanic/Old French).

**Lorne** a Scottish placename (the northern area of Argyll), of uncertain meaning, used as a first name; a variant form is *Lorn*.

**Lot** a veil; a covering (Hebrew).

**Louis** the French form of Lewis; diminutive forms are *Lou, Louie*.

**Lovel, Lovell** a surname, meaning little wolf, used as a first name (Old French); a variant form is *Lowell*.

**Lucan** a placename, meaning place of elms, used as

a first name (Irish Gaelic).
**Lucian** belonging to or sprung from Lucius (Latin).
**Lucius** from lux, light (Latin).
**Luke** of Lucania in Italy (Latin).
**Luther** illustrious warrior (Germanic).
**Lyle** a variant form of Lisle.
**Lynden, Lyndon** a surname, meaning dweller by lime trees, used as a first name; a diminutive form is *Lyn*.
**Lynn** a surname, meaning pool or waterfall, used as a first name (Celtic); diminutive forms are *Lyn, Lin, Linn*.
**Lysander** liberator (Greek); a diminutive form is *Sandy*.

**Maahir** skilled (Indian).
**Madin** delightful (Indian), a surname, meaning son of Matthew or Maud, used as a first name (Old English).
**Madhav** Krishna (Hindu).
**Madoc** good; beneficent (Welsh).
**Magan** absorbed (Indian).
**Magee** a surname, meaning son of Hugh, used a first name (Irish Gaelic).
**Magnus** great (Latin).

**Malachi** messenger of Jehovah (Hebrew).
**Malcolm** servant of Columba (Scots Gaelic); diminutive forms are *Calum, Mal*.
**Malise** servant of Jesus (Scots Gaelic).
**Mallory** a surname, meaning unfortunate, luckless, used as a first name (Old French).
**Malone** a surname, meaning follower of St John, sometimes used as a first name (Irish Gaelic).
**Mandhatri** prince (Hindu).
**Manfred** man of peace (Germanic); a diminutive form is *Manny*.
**Manley** a surname, meaning brave, upright, used as a first name (Middle English).
**Manuel** the Spanish form of Emmanuel.
**Marcus** the Latin form of Mark, now used as an English variant form; a variant form is *Marc*.
**Marius** martial (Latin).
**Mark** a hammer; a male; sprung from Mars (Latin); variant forms are *Marcus, Marcius*.
**Markandeya** a sage (Hindu).
**Marland** a surname, meaning lake land, used as a first name (Old English).
**Marlon** of uncertain meaning, possibly hawk-like (French).
**Marlow** a placename and

surname, meaning land of the former pool, used as a first name (Old English); variant forms are *Marlo, Marlowe*.

**Marmaduke** a mighty noble; Madoc's servant (Celtic); a diminutive form is *Duke*.

**Marmion** a surname, meaning brat, monkey, used as a first name (Old French).

**Marsden** a surname, meaning boundary valley, used as a first name (Old English).

**Marsh** a surname, meaning marsh, used as a first name (Old English).

**Marshall** a surname, meaning horse servant, used as a first name (Germanic).

**Marston** a surname, meaning place by a marsh, used as a first name (Old English).

**Martin** of Mars; warlike (Latin); a variant form is *Martyn*; a diminutive form is *Marty*.

**Mather** a surname, meaning mower, used as a first name (Old English).

**Matheson, Mathieson** a surname, meaning son of Matthew, used as a first name.

**Matthew** gift of Jehovah (Hebrew); diminutive forms are *Mat, Matt, Mattie*.

**Matthias** a Latin form of Matthew; a variant form is *Mathias*.

**Maurice** Moorish, dark-coloured (Latin); a diminutive form is *Mo*.

**Max** a diminutive form of Maximilian, Maxwell, also used independently; a diminutive form is *Maxie*.

**Maximilian** the greatest, a combination of Maximus and Aemilianus (Latin); diminutive forms are *Max, Maxie*.

**Maxwell** a surname, meaning spring of Magnus, used as a first name; a diminutive form is *Max*.

**Mayer** a surname, meaning physician (Old French) or farmer (Germanic), used as a first name; variant forms are *Meyer, Myer*.

**Maynard** a surname, meaning strong, brave, used as a first name (Germanic).

**Mayo** a placename, meaning plain of the yew tree, used as a first name (Irish Gaelic).

**Medwin** a surname, meaning mead friend, used as a first name (Old English).

**Melville, Melvin, Melvyn** a surname, meaning Amalo's place, used as a first name (Old French); a diminutive form is *Mel*.

**Meredith** a surname, meaning lord, used as a first name (Welsh).

**Merfyn** eminent matter (Welsh).

**Merle** blackbird (Old French); a variant form of Meriel.

**Merlin, Merlyn** sea fort (Welsh).

**Merrill** a surname, meaning son of Muriel (Celtic) or pleasant place (Old English), used as a first name; variant forms are *Meryl, Merryll*.

**Merton** a surname, meaning farmstead by the pool, used as a first name (Old English).

**Mervin, Mervyn** a surname, meaning famous friend, used as a first name (Old English); a variant form is *Marvin*; anglicized forms of Merfyn.

**Michael** who is like unto God? (Hebrew); diminutive forms are *Mick, Micky, Mike*.

**Miles** a soldier (Germanic); a variant form is *Myles*.

**Milton** a surname, meaning middle farmstead or mill farm, used as a first name (Old English); a diminutive form is *Milt*.

**Milward** a surname, meaning mill keeper, used as a first name (Old English); a variant form is *Millward*.

**Mitchell** a surname form of Michael meaning big, great; used as a first name (Old English).

**Modred** counsellor; in Arthurian legend the knight who killed King Arthur (Old English).

**Mohan** charming (Hindu).

**Monroe, Monro** a surname, meaning mouth of the Roe river, used as a first name (Irish Gaelic); variant forms are *Munro, Munroe, Munrow*.

**Montague, Montagu** a surname, meaning pointed hill, used as a first name; a diminutive form is *Monty*.

**Montgomery, Montgomerie** a surname, meaning hill of powerful man, used as a first name (Old French/Germanic); a diminutive form is *Monty*.

**Morgan** sea-dweller (Celtic).

**Mortimer** a surname, meaning dead sea, used as a first name (Old French).

**Morton** a surname, meaning farmstead moor, used as a first name (Old English).

**Moses** meaning uncertain, most probably an Egyptian name (Hebrew).

**Muir** a Scottish form of the surname Moore, meaning moor (Old French), used as a first name.

**Mungo** amiable (Gaelic).

**Murdo, Murdoch** sea-warrior (Scots Gaelic).

**Murray** a surname, meaning seaboard place used as a first name; a variant form is *Moray*.

**Myer** a surname, meaning marsh (Old Norse), used as a first name; a variant form of Mayer.

**Myron** fragrant oil (Greek).

# N

**Nairn** dweller by the alder tree (Celtic).

**Nash** a surname, meaning ash tree, used as a first name (Old English).

**Nathan** gift (Hebrew); a diminutive form is *Nat*.

**Nathaniel, Nathanael** God gave (Hebrew); a diminutive form is *Nat*.

**Neel** blue (Hindu).

**Neil** champion (Gaelic); variant forms are *Neal, Neale, Nial, Niall*.

**Nelson** a surname, meaning son of Neil, used as a first name.

**Nero** dark, black-haired (Latin).

**Nestor** coming home (Greek).

**Neven** a variant form of Nevin.

**Neville** a placename and surname, meaning new place, used as a first name (Old French).

**Nevin** a surname, meaning little saint, used as a first name (Irish Gaelic); variant form is Niven.

**Newland** a surname, meaning new land, used as a first name (Old English).

**Newlyn, Newlin** a placename and surname, meaning pool for a fleet, used as a first name (Cornish).

**Nicholas** victory of the people (Greek); a variant form is *Nicolas*; diminutive forms are *Nick, Nicky*.

**Nicol** a Scottish surname form of Nicholas used as a first name.

**Nigel** black (Latin).

**Ninian** meaning uncertain; the name of a 5th-century saint (Celtic).

**Nixon** a surname, meaning the son of Nicholas, used as a first name; a variant form is *Nickson*.

**Noah** rest (Hebrew).

**Noble** a surname, meaning noble, famous, used as a first name (Old French).

**Noël, Noel** Christmas (French).

**Nolan** a surname, meaning son of the champion, used as a first name (Irish Gaelic).

**Norman** northman (Germanic); a diminutive form is *Norrie*.

**Northcliffe** a surname, meaning north cliff, used as a first name (Old English).

**Norton** a surname, meaning northern farmstead or village, used as a surname (Old English).

**Norwood** a surname, meaning north wood, used as a first name (Old English).

**Nowell** an English form of Noël.

# O

**Oakley** a surname, meaning oak tree meadow, used as a first name (Old English).

**Ogden** a surname, meaning oak valley, used as a first name (Old English).

**Ogilvie** a surname, meaning high peak, used as a first name (Celtic).

**Olaf, Olav** divine remnant (Old Norse).

**Oliver** an olive tree (Latin); diminutive forms are *Ollie, Olly, Noll, Nollie*.

**Omar** first son (Arabic), life, long living (Indian).

**Omeir** long living (Indian).

**Orion** son of light (Greek).

**Orlando** the Italian form of Roland.

**Ormond, Ormonde** a surname, meaning from east Munster, used as a first name (Irish Gaelic).

**Orpheus** of uncertain meaning; in Greek mythology, a poet who sought to retrieve his wife Eurydice from Hades.

**Orson** little bear (Latin).

**Orville, Orvil** golden place (Old French).

**Osbert** god-bright (Old English); a diminutive form is *Ossie*.

**Osborn, Osborne, Osbourne** a surname, meaning divine bear, or warrior, used as a first name (Germanic) a diminutive form is *Ossie*.

**Oscar** divine spear (Germanic); a diminutive form is *Ossie*.

**Osmond, Osmund** divine protection (Germanic); a diminutive form is *Ossie*.

**Oswald** divine rule (Germanic).

**Oswin** god-friend (Old English).

**Otis** a surname, meaning son of Ote, used as a first name (Germanic).

**Otto** rich (Germanic).

**Owain** a Welsh form of Eugene.

**Owen** a lamb; a young warrior (Celtic).

**Oxford** a placename, meaning ford for oxen, used as a first name (Old English).

# P

**Pablo** the Spanish form of Paul.

**Padraig** the Irish Gaelic form of Patrick.

**Paolo** the Italian form of Paul.

**Pascal** of the passover (Latin/French).

**Patrick** noble; a patrician (Latin); a variant form is *Patric*.

**Paul** little (Latin).

**Pavan** sacred (Indian).

**Peregrine** wanderer (Latin); a diminutive form is *Perry*.

**Perry** diminutive form of Peregrine, now used in its own right; a surname, meaning pear tree, used as a first name (Old English).

**Peter** stone (Latin); the diminutive form is *Pete*.

**Petrus** a German form of Peter.

**Phalak** sky (Indian).

**Phelim** always good (Irish).

**Philbert** very bright (Germanic).

**Philemon** friendly (Greek).

**Philip** lover of horses (Greek); a variant form is *Phillip*; diminutive forms are *Phil, Pip*.

**Phineas, Phinehas** serpent's mouth (Hebrew).

**Pierre** the French form of Peter.

**Piers** a variant form of Peter.

**Pius** holy (Latin).

**Placido** peaceful (Latin/Spanish).

**Plato** broad (Greek).

**Presley** a surname, meaning priests' meadow, used as a first name.

# Q

**Qasim** divider (Indian).

**Qatadah** a hardwood tree (Indian).

**Qays** firm (Indian).

**Qudamah** courage (Indian).

**Quentin** fifth (Latin); a variant form is *Quinton*.

**Quigley, Quigly** a surname, meaning untidy, used as a first name (Irish Gaelic).

**Quincy, Quincey** a surname, meaning fifth place, used as a first name (Latin/French).

**Quinlan** well formed (Irish Gaelic).

**Quinn** a surname, meaning wise, used as a first name (Irish Gaelic).

**Quintus** fifth (Latin).

**Qutaybah** irritable, impatient (Indian).

# R

**Raban** raven (Germanic).

**Radcliffe** a surname, meaning red cliff, used as a first name (Old English).

**Radley** a surname, meaning red meadow, used as a first name (Old English).

**Radnor** a placename and surname, meaning red slopes, used as a first name (Old English).

**Rafferty** a surname, meaning prosperous, used as a first name (Irish Gaelic).

**Rainier** a French form of Rayner.

**Raleigh** a surname, meaning red or deer meadow, sometimes used as a first name (Old English); variant forms are *Rawley, Rayleigh*.

**Ralph** famous wolf or hero (Germanic); variant forms are *Rafe, Rolph*.

**Ram** height (Hebrew).

**Ramón** a Spanish form of Raymond.

**Ramsay, Ramsey** a placename and surname, meaning wild garlic, river island, used as a first name (Old Norse).

**Ramsden** Ram's valley (Old English).

**Ranald** a variant form of Reginald.

**Randal, Randall** a surname, diminutive form of Randolph used as a first name (Old English); a variant form is *Ranulf*.

**Randolf, Randolph** shield-wolf (Germanic); a variant form is

*Ranulf;* diminutive forms are *Rand, Randy*.

**Randy** a diminutive form of Randolf, also used independently.

**Rankin, Rankine** a diminutive surname form of Randolph used as a first name.

**Ransom** a surname, meaning son of Rand, used as a first name.

**Ranulf** a variant form of Randolf.

**Raoul** the French form of Ralph.

**Raphael** the healing of God (Hebrew).

**Ray** a diminutive form of Raymond, now used independently; a variant form is *Rae*.

**Raymond, Raymund** wise protection (Germanic); a diminutive form is *Ray*.

**Rayne** a surname, meaning mighty army, used as a first name; a variant form is *Rayner*.

**Rayner** a variant form of Rayne (Germanic).

**Read, Reade** a surname, meaning red-headed, used as a first name (Old English); variant forms are *Reed, Reede*.

**Reading** a placename and surname, meaning people of the red one, used as a first name; a variant form is *Redding*.

**Reagan** a variant form of Regan.

**Reardon** a variant form of Riordan.

**Redman** a surname, meaning red cairn or thatcher, used as a first name (Old English); a variant form of Redmond.

**Redmond** counsel protection (Germanic); a variant form is *Redman*.

**Reece** a surname form of Rhys used as a first name.

**Rees** the English form of Rhys.

**Reeve, Reeves** steward, bailiff (Old English).

**Regan** a surname, meaning little king, used as a first name (Irish Gaelic); variant forms are *Reagan, Rogan*.

**Reginald** counsel rule (Germanic); diminutive forms are *Reg, Reggie*.

**Reilly** a surname, meaning valiant, used as a first name (Irish Gaelic); a variant form is *Riley*.

**Remus** power (Latin).

**Renaldo** a Spanish form of Reginald.

**Renato** an Italian and Spanish form of Reginald.

**Renault** a French form of Reginald.

**René** born again (French).

**Renfrew** a placename and surname, meaning point of the torrent, used as a first name (Celtic).

**Renton** a surname, meaning farmstead of Power, used as a first name (Old English).

**Reuben** behold a son (Hebrew); a diminutive form is *Rube*.

**Rex** king (Latin).

**Reynard** brave advice (Germanic); fox (French).

**Reynold** strong rule (Germanic).

**Rhodri** circle ruler (Welsh).

**Rhys** ardour (Welsh).

**Ricardo** a Spanish form of Richard.

**Richard** a strong king; powerful (Germanic); diminutive forms are *Dick, Rich, Richey, Richie, Rick, Rickie, Ricky, Ritchie*.

**Richmond** a surname, meaning strong hill, used as a first name (Old French); diminutive forms are *Rich, Richey, Richie*.

**Rider** a surname, meaning knight, rider, used as a first name (Old English).

**Ritchie** a diminutive and surname form of Richard.

**Roald** famous ruler (Old Norse).

**Robert** bright in fame (Germanic); diminutive forms are *Bob, Bobby, Rab, Rob, Robbie, Robby, Robin*.

**Robin** a diminutive form of Robert, now used independently; a variant form is *Robyn*.

**Robinson** a surname, meaning son of Robert, used as a first name (Old English).

**Rocco** of uncertain meaning,

possibly crow (Germanic).

**Roderick, Roderic** fame, powerful (Germanic); diminutive forms are *Rod, Roddy, Rurik*.

**Roderico** an Italian form of Roderick.

**Rodney** from a reed island (Old English); diminutive forms are *Rod, Roddy*.

**Rodrigo** an Italian and Spanish form of Roderick.

**Roger** famous with the spear (Germanic); a variant form is *Rodger*.

**Rohan** healing, incense (Sanskrit), ascending (Indian).

**Roland** fame of the land (Germanic); variant forms are Rolland, Rowland; a diminutive form is *Roly*.

**Rolf** a contraction of Rudolf; a variant form is *Rollo*.

**Romeo** a Roman (Latin).

**Ronald** a variant form of Reginald; diminutive forms are *Ron, Ronnie, Ronny*.

**Ronan** little seal (Irish Gaelic).

**Rooney** red, red-complexioned (Gaelic).

**Rory** red (Irish and Scots Gaelic).

**Roscoe** a surname, meaning deer wood, used as a first name (Old Norse).

**Ross** a placename and surname, meaning promontory or moorland, used as a first name (Scots Gaelic).

**Rowan** red (Irish Gaelic).

**Roy** red (Gaelic); king (Old French).

**Royal** a variant form of Royle.

**Royle** a surname, meaning rye hill, used as a first name (Old English); a variant form is *Royal*.

**Royston** a surname, meaning place of Royce, now used as a first name (Germanic/Old English).

**Rudolf, Rudolph** famous wolf; hero (Germanic).

**Rudyard** reed enclosure (Old English).

**Rufus** red-haired (Latin); a diminutive form is *Rufe*.

**Rugby** a placename and surname, meaning Hroca's stronghold, used as a first name (Old English).

**Rupert** an anglicized Germanic form of Robert.

**Russell** a surname, meaning red hair, used as a first name (Old French); a diminutive form is *Russ*.

**Ruy** a Spanish form of Roderick.

**Ryan** the Irish surname of uncertain meaning used as a first name.

**Rye** from the riverbank (French).

**Rylan, Ryland** a surname, meaning where rye grows, used as a first name (Old English).

# S

**Saabir** patient (Indian).

**Sabino** an Italian form of Sabinus.

**Sabinus** Sabine man (Latin); a shortened form is *Sabin*.

**Safal** succeed (Indian).

**Salomo** a Dutch and German form of Solomon.

**Salvador** Christ the saviour (Latin/Spanish).

**Salvatore** the Italian form of Salvador.

**Sam** a diminutive form of Samuel, now used independently.

**Samir** wind (Hindu).

**Samson, Sampson** like the sun (Hebrew).

**Samuel** name of God, or heard by God (Hebrew); diminutive forms are *Sam, Sammy*.

**Sancho** holy (Spanish).

**Sanders** from Alexander (Old English); a diminutive form is *Sandy*.

**Sanford** a surname, meaning sandy ford, used as a first name (Old English).

**Santo** saint (Italian).

**Satyak** honest (Indian).

**Satyavrat** king (Hindu).

**Saul** asked for by God (Hebrew).

**Saumya** handsome (Indian).

**Saurabh** fragrant (Indian).

**Saurav** melodious (Indian).

**Saveur** the French form of Salvador.

**Savit** sun (Indian).

**Saxon** people of the short swords (Germanic).

**Scott** a surname, meaning of Scotland, used as a first name.

**Seamas, Seamus** Irish Gaelic forms of James.

**Sean** an Irish Gaelic form of John.

**Searle** a surname, meaning armed warrior, used as a first name (Germanic).

**Seaton** a placename and surname, meaning farmstead at the sea, used as a first name (Old English); a variant form is *Seton*.

**Sebastian** august, majestic (Greek).

**Secondo** the Italian form of Secundus.

**Secundus** second born (Latin).

**Seeley** a first name, meaning blessed and happy, used as a first name (Old English); a variant form is *Sealey*.

**Selby** a placename and surname, meaning place by the willow trees, used as a first name (Old English).

**Selden** from the valley of the willow tree (Old English).

**Selig** blessed, happy one (Yiddish); a variant form is *Zelig*.

**Selwyn, Selwin** wild (Germanic).

**Senior** a surname, meaning lord, used as a first name (Old French); a variant form is *Seigneur*.

**Septimus** seventh (Latin).

**Serge** the French form of Sergius.

**Sergei** the Russian form of Sergius.

**Sergio** the Italian form of Sergius.

**Sergius** a Roman family name of Etruscan origin and unknown meaning.

**Sesto** the Italian form of Sextus.

**Seth** appointed (Hebrew).

**Seumas** a Gaelic form of James.

**Sewald, Sewall, Sewell,** a surname, meaning sea powerful, used as a first name (Old English); a variant form is *Siwald*.

**Sexton** a surname, meaning sacristan, used as a first name (Old French).

**Sextus** sixth (Latin).

**Seymour** a surname, meaning from Saint-Maur in France, used as a first name (Old French).

**Shalom** peace (Hebrew).

**Shamus** an anglicized form of Seamus.

**Shane** an anglicized form of Sean.

**Shanley** a surname, meaning son of the hero, used as a first name (Irish Gaelic).

**Shardul** the best (Indian).

**Shashwat** everlasting (Hindu).

**Shaw** a surname, meaning small wood or grove, used as a first name (Old English).

**Shawn, Shaun** anglicized forms of Sean.

**Shea** a surname, meaning stately, dauntless, used as a first name (Irish Gaelic).

**Sheffield** a placename, meaning open land by the Sheaf river, used as a first name (Old English).

**Sheldon** a surname, meaning heathery hill with a shed, flat-topped hill, or steep valley, used as a first name (Old English).

**Shepard** a surname, meaning sheep herder, shepherd, used as a first name (Old English).

**Sherborne, Sherbourne** a surname, meaning clear stream, used as a first name (Old English).

**Sheridan** a surname, meaning seeking, used as a first name (Irish Gaelic).

**Sherlock** fair-haired (Old English).

**Sherman** a surname, meaning shearman, used as a first name (Old English).

**Sherwin** a surname, meaning loyal friend or fast-footed, used as a first name (Old English).

**Sherwood** a placename and surname, meaning shore wood, used as a first name (Old English).

**Sholto** sower, seed-bearing (Scots Gaelic).

**Siddall, Siddell** a surname, meaning broad slope, used as a first name (Old English).

**Sidney** a surname, meaning wide island, used as a first name; a variant form is *Sydney*; a diminutive form is *Sid*.

**Siegfried** victory peace (Germanic).

**Sigiswald** victorious ruler (Germanic).

**Sigmund** victory protection (Germanic); a diminutive form is *Sig*.

**Sigurd** victorious guardian (Old Norse).

**Silas** a shortened form of Silvanus.

**Silvain** a French form of Silvanus.

**Silvanus** of a wood (Latin); a variant form is Sylvanus.

**Silvester** of a wood (Latin); a variant form is *Sylvester*; a diminutive form is *Sly*.

**Silvio** the Italian and Spanish forms of Silvanus.

**Simon, Simeon** hearing with acceptance (Hebrew); diminutive forms are *Sim, Simmy*.

**Sinha** hero (Indian).

**Sinclair** a surname, meaning from St Clair in France, used as a first name (Old French); a variant form is *St Clair*.

**Skelton** a surname, meaning farmstead on a hill, used as first name (Old English).

**Skerry** sea rock (Old Norse).

**Skipper** a nickname and surname, meaning jumping (Middle English) or ship's captain (Dutch), used as a first name; a diminutive form is *Skip*.

**Skipton** a placename and surname, meaning sheep farm, used as a first name (Old English).

**Slade** a surname, meaning valley, used as a first name (Old English).

**Sly** a diminutive form of Silvester, Sylvester.

**Smith** a surname, meaning blacksmith, used as a first name (Old English).

**Snowden, Snowdon** a surname, meaning snowy hill, used as a first name (Old English).

**Sohan** handsome (Indian).

**Sohil** beautiful (Indian).

**Sol** the sun (Latin); a diminutive form of Solomon.

**Solomon** peaceable (Hebrew); diminutive forms are Sol, Solly.

**Somerled** summer traveller (Old Norse).

**Somerset** a placename, meaning settlers around the summer farmstead, used as a first name (Old English).

**Somerton** a placename, meaning summer farmstead, used as a first name (Old English).

**Somhairle** an Irish and Scots Gaelic form of Somerled.

**Sorley** an anglicized form of Somhairle.

**Sorrel** sour (Germanic), the name of a salad plant used as a first name.

**Sourish** Lord Vishnu (Indian).

**Spencer** a surname, meaning steward or dispenser, used as a first name (Old French).

**Squire** a surname, meaning shield bearer, used as a first name (Old French).

**Sridatta** given by God (Indian).

**St John** Saint John (pronounced sinjun).

**Stacey** a diminutive form of Eustace, now used independently.

**Stafford** a surname, meaning ford by a landing place, used as a first name (Old English).

**Standish** a surname, meaning stony pasture, used as a first name (Old English).

**Stanford** a surname, meaning stone ford, used as a first name (Old English); a variant form is *Stamford*.

**Stanhope** a surname, meaning stony hollow, used as a first name (Old English).

**Stanislas, Stanislaus** government and glory (Slavonic).

**Stanley** a surname and placename meaning stony field, used as a first name (Old English).

**Stanton** a surname, meaning stony farmstead, used as a first name (Old English).

**Stephen, Steven** crown (Greek); diminutive forms are *Stefan, Steve, Stevie*.

**Sterling** a surname, meaning little star, used as a first name (Old English); a variant form is *Stirling*.

**Stewart** a variant and surname form of Stuart.

**Sthavir** Lord Brahma (Indian).

**Stirling** a variant form of Sterling; a placename, meaning enclosed land by the stream, used as a first name (Scottish Gaelic).

**Stockland** a surname, meaning

land of a religious house, used as a first name (Old English).

**Stockley** a surname, meaning cleared meadow of a religious house, used as a first name (Old English).

**Stockton** a placename and surname, meaning outlying farmstead, used as a first name (Old English).

**Stoddard** a surname, meaning horse keeper, used as a first name (Old English).

**Stoke** a placename and surname, meaning outlying farmstead, used as a first name (Old English).

**Stowe** a surname, meaning holy place, used as a first name (Old English).

**Strachan, Strahan** a surname, meaning little valley, used as a first name (Scots Gaelic).

**Stratford** a placename, meaning ford on a Roman road, used as a first name (Old English).

**Stuart, Stewart, Steuart** the surname meaning steward used as a first name (Old English).

**Suchendra** Lord of piousness (Indian).

**Sukumar** tender (Hindu).

**Sullivan** a surname, meaning black-eyed, used as a first name (Irish Gaelic).

**Sumner** a surname, meaning one who summons, used as a first name (Old French).

**Surya** the sun (Hindu).

**Sutherland** a placename and surname, meaning southern land, used as a first name (Old Norse).

**Sutton** a placename and surname, meaning southern farmstead, used as a first name (Old English).

**Svarg** heaven (Indian).

**Sven** lad (Old Norse).

**Swastik** auspicious (Indian).

**Syon** gentle (Indian).

# T

**Tad** a diminutive form of Thaddeus, also used independently.

**Tadhg** an Irish Gaelic form of Thaddeus; a variant form is *Teague*.

**Taffy** Welsh form of David (Celtic).

**Taggart** a surname, meaning priest, used as a first name (Scots Gaelic).

**Talbot** a surname, meaning command of the valley, used as a first name (Germanic).

**Tancred** thought strong (Germanic).

**Tarang** wave (Indian).

**Tareef** rare (Indian).

**Tarendra** prince of stars (Indian).

**Tarfah** kind of tree (Indian).

**Tariq** name of a star (Indian).

**Tate** a surname, meaning cheerful, used as a first name (Old Norse); variant forms are *Tait, Teyte*.

**Tawfeeq** success, reconciliation (Indian).

**Taylor** a surname, meaning tailor, used as a first name (Old French).

**Taymullah** servant of God (Indian).

**Tebaldo** an Italian form of Theobold.

**Tejas** light (Indian).

**Tennison, Tennyson** variant forms of Dennison.

**Teobaldo** an Italian and Spanish form of Theobald.

**Terence** from a Roman family name of unknown origin (Latin); variant forms are *Terrance, Terrence*; diminutive forms are *Tel, Terry*.

**Terris, Terriss** a surname, meaning son of Terence, used as a first name.

**Tertius** third (Latin).

**Teyte** a variant form of Tait.

**Thaddeus** gift of God (Greek-Aramaic); diminutive forms are *Tad, Thad, Thaddy*.

**Thaabit** firm (Indian).

**Thaine** a surname, meaning holder of land in return for military service, used as a first name (Old English); a variant form is *Thane*.

**Thaqib** shooting star (Indian).

**Theobald** bold for the people (Germanic); a diminutive form is *Theo*.

**Theodore** the gift of God (Greek); diminutive forms are *Ted, Teddie, Teddy, Theo*.

**Theodoric, Theodorick** people powerful (Germanic); diminutive forms are *Derek, Derrick, Dirk, Ted, Teddie, Teddy*.

**Theophilus** lover of God (Greek).

**Theron** hero (Greek).

**Thewlis** a surname, meaning ill-mannered, used as a first name (Old English).

**Thierry** a French form of Theodoric.

**Thomas** twin (Aramaic); diminutive forms are *Tam, Thom, Tom, Tommy*.

**Thor** thunder (Old Norse), in Norse mythology, the god of thunder; a variant form is *Tor*.

**Thorburn** a surname, meaning Thor's warrior or bear, used as a first name (Old Norse).

**Thorndike, Thorndyke** a surname, meaning thorny ditch, used as a first name (Old English).

**Thorne** a surname, meaning thorn tree or hawthorn, used as a first name (Old English).

**Thorold** Thor rule (Old Norse); a variant form is *Torold*.

**Thorp, Thorpe** a surname, meaning farm village, used as a first name (Old English).

**Thorwald** ruled by Thor (Old Norse); a variant form is *Torvald*.

**Thurstan, Thurston** a surname, meaning Thor stone, used as a first name (Old Norse).

**Tiernan, Tierney** a surname, meaning lord, used as a first name (Irish Gaelic); a variant form is *Kiernan*.

**Till** a German diminutive form of Dietrich.

**Timon** reward (Greek).

**Timothy** honouring God (Greek); diminutive forms are *Tim, Timmie, Timmy*.

**Titian** an English form of Titianus.

**Titianus** a Roman name derived from *Titus*.

**Tito** the Italian and Spanish form of Titus.

**Titus** protected (Latin).

**Tobias, Tobiah** Jehovah is good (Hebrew); a diminutive form is *Toby*.

**Todd** a surname, meaning fox, used as a first name (Old Norse).

**Todhunter** a surname, meaning foxhunter, used as a first name (Old Norse/Old English).

**Tony** a diminutive form of Antony.

**Tor** a variant form of Thor.

**Tormod** Thor's spirit (Old Norse).

**Torold** a variant form of Thorold.

**Torquil** God's cauldron (Old Norse).

**Torr** a surname, meaning tower (Old English) or bull (Old French) used as a first name.

**Torvald** a variant form of Thorwald.

**Townsend, Townshend** a surname, meaning end of the village, used as a first name (Old English).

**Tracey** a variant form of Tracy.

**Tracy** a surname, meaning Thracian, used as a first name (Old French); a variant form is *Tracey*.

**Traherne** a surname, meaning iron strength, used as a first name (Welsh).

**Travers** a surname, meaning crossing, crossroads, used as a first name (Old French); a variant form is *Travis*.

**Tremaine, Tremayne** a

surname, meaning homestead on the rock, used as a first name (Cornish).

**Trent** a river name, meaning liable to flood, used as a first name (Celtic).

**Trevelyan** a surname, meaning mill farm, used as a first name (Cornish).

**Trevor** a surname, meaning big river, used as a first name (Welsh); a diminutive form is *Trev*.

**Tristram** grave; pensive (Celtic).

**Tristan** tumult (Celtic).

**Troy** a surname, meaning of Troyes, used as a first name (Old French); the name of the city in Asia Minor besieged by the Greeks used as a first name.

**True** the adjective for the quality of being faithful and loyal, used as a first name.

**Truelove** a surname, meaning faithful sweetheart, used as a first name (Old English).

**Trueman, Truman** a surname, meaning faithful servant, used as a first name (Old English).

**Trystan** a Welsh form of Tristan.

**Tudor** a Welsh form of Theodore.

**Tullio** the Italian form of Tullius.

**Tullius** a Roman family name of Etruscan origin and uncertain meaning.

**Tully** a surname, meaning flood, used as a first name (Irish Gaelic); an English form of Tullius.

**Turag** a thought (Indian).

**Turner** a surname, meaning worker on a lathe, used as a first name (Old French).

**Turpin** a surname, meaning Thor the Finn, used as a first name (Old Norse).

**Tushar** winter (Indian).

**Twyford** a surname, meaning double ford, used as a first name (Old English).

**Tybalt** a variant form of Theobald; a diminutive form is *Ty*.

**Tye** a surname, meaning enclosure, used as a first name (Old English).

**Tyler** a surname, meaning tile-maker, used as a first name (Old English); a diminutive form is *Ty*.

**Tyrone** a placename and surname, meaning land of Owen, used as a first name (Irish Gaelic); a diminutive form is *Ty*.

**Tyson** a surname, meaning fire-brand, used as a first name (Old French).

# U

**Uberto** an Italian form of Hubert.

**Uday** sunrise (Indian).

**Udo** prosperous (Germanic).

**Ugo, Ugolino, Ugone** Italian forms of Hugh.

**Ulmar, Ulmer** wolf (Old English).

**Ulric, Ulrick** wolf power (Old English); the English form of Ulrich.

**Ulrich** fortune and power (Germanic).

**Ulysses** wrathful (Greek); a diminutive form is *Lyss.*

**Umang** happiness (Indian).

**Umberto** the Italian form of Humbert.

**Unmesh** eternal happiness, joy (Indian).

**Unnabh** highest (Indian).

**Unwin** a surname, meaning not a friend, used as a first name (Old English).

**Upendra** an element (Hindu).

**Urav** excitement (Indian).

**Urban** town-dweller (Latin).

**Uri** light (Hebrew).

**Uriah** fire of the Lord (Hebrew).

**Urian** a husbandman (Danish).

**Uriel** light of God (Hebrew).

**Urjavaha** of the Nimi dynasty (Hindu).

**Urvang** mountain (Indian).

**Urvish** Lord of the earth (Indian).

**Utkarsh** high quality (Indian).

**Uttam** best (Indian).

**Uzziah** Jehovah is strength (Hebrew).

**Uzziel** God is strength (Hebrew).

# V

**Vachel** little calf (Old French).

**Valdemar** a variant form of Waldemar.

**Valentine** strong; healthy; powerful (Latin); a diminutive form is *Val.*

**Valentino** an Italian form of Valentine.

**Valerian** form of Valerie.

**Valéry** foreign power (Germanic).

**Vasili, Vassily** Russian forms of Basil.

**Vaughan, Vaughn** a surname, meaning small one, used as a first name (Welsh).

**Vere** a surname, meaning from

Ver in France, used as a first name (Old French).

**Vernon** a surname, meaning alder tree, used as a first name (Old French).

**Vibhor** ecstatic (Indian).

**Vicente** a Spanish form of Vincent.

**Victor** conqueror (Latin); a diminutive form is *Vic*.

**Vidal** a Spanish form of vitalis (Latin), living, vital.

**Vijay** victor (Hindu).

**Vilhelm** a Swedish form of William.

**Vinay** good behaviour (Hindu).

**Vincent** conquering; victorious (Latin); diminutive forms are *Vince, Vinnie, Vinny*.

**Vitore** an Italian form of Victor.

**Vittorio** an Italian form of Victor.

**Vladimir** royally famous (Slavonic).

**Vladislav** great ruler (Slavonic).

**Vrajesh** Lord Krishna (Indian).

**Vrishab** excellent (Indian).

# W

**Waahid** unequalled (Indian).

**Wade** a surname, meaning to go, or at the ford, used as a first name (Old English).

**Wadee** calm, peaceful (Indian).

**Wainwright** a surname, meaning maker of carts, used as a first name (Old English).

**Wajeeh** noble (Indian).

**Wake** a surname, meaning alert, used as a first name (Old English).

**Waldemar** noted ruler (Germanic); a variant form is *Valdemar*.

**Waldo** ruler (Germanic).

**Waleed** newborn child (Indian).

**Walker** a surname, meaning a fuller, used as a first name (Old English).

**Wallace** a Scots variant form of Wallis; a diminutive form is *Wally*.

**Wallis** a man who comes from Wales (Old English); a variant form is *Wallace*; a diminutive form is *Wally*.

**Waliyullah** supporter of God (Indian).

**Wally** a diminutive form of Wallace, Wallis.

**Walt** a diminutive form of Walter, Walton.

**Walter** ruler of army, people (Germanic); diminutive forms are *Walt, Wat, Watty*.

**Walther** a German form of Walter.

**Walton** a surname, meaning

farmstead of the Britons, used as a first name (Old English); a diminutive form is *Walt*.

**Ward** a surname, meaning watchman; guard, used as a first name (Old English).

**Warne** a surname, meaning alder wood, used as a first name (Cornish).

**Warner** a surname, meaning protecting army, used as a first name (Germanic).

**Warren** a surname, meaning wasteland or game park, used as a first name (Old French).

**Warwick** a placename and surname, meaning dwellings by the weir, used as a first name (Old English).

**Washington** a placename and surname, meaning Wassa's estate, used as a first name (Old English).

**Waseem** graceful, good looking (Indian).

**Wat, Watty** a diminutive form of Walter.

**Waverley** a placename, meaning meadow or clearing by the swampy ground, used as a first name (Old English).

**Wayne** a surname, meaning a carter, used as a first name.

**Webster** a surname, meaning woman weaver, used as a first name (Old English).

**Wellington** a placename and surname, meaning Weola's farmstead, used as a first name (Old English).

**Wenceslaus, Wenceslas** wreathed with glory (Slavonic).

**Wendel, Wendell** of the Wend people (Germanic); a variant form is Wendel.

**Wentworth** a surname, meaning winter enclosure, used as a first name (Old English).

**Werner** a German form of Warner.

**Wesley** a surname, meaning west wood, used as a first name (Old English); a diminutive form is Wes.

**Whitaker** a surname, meaning white acre, used as a first name (Old English); a variant form is *Whittaker*.

**Whitman** a surname, meaning white- or fair-haired, used as a first name (Old English).

**Whitney** a surname and placename, meaning white island or Witta's island, used as a first name (Old English).

**Whittaker** a variant form of Whitaker.

**Wilbert** well-born (Old English).

**Wilbur** wild boar (Old English).

**Wilfrid, Wilfred** will peace (Germanic); a diminutive form is *Wilf*.

**Wilhelm** the German form of

William; a diminutive form is *Wim*.

**Will, Willie, Willy** diminutive forms of William.

**Willard** a surname, meaning bold resolve, used as a first name (Old English).

**Willemot** resolute in spirit (Germanic).

**William** resolute helmet (Germanic); diminutive forms are *Bill, Will*.

**Willoughby** a surname, meaning farm by the willows, used as a first name (Old Norse/Old English).

**Willson** a variant form of Wilson.

**Wilmer** famous will or desire (Old English).

**Wilmot** a diminutive surname form of William.

**Wilson** a surname, meaning son of Will, used as a first name (Old English); a variant form is *Willson*.

**Wim** a contraction of Wilhelm.

**Windham** a variant form of Wyndham.

**Winston** a placename and surname, meaning friend's place or farm, used as a first name (Old English).

**Winton** a surname, meaning friend's farm, used as a first name (Old English).

**Wolf, Wolfe** wolf (Old English).

**Wolfgang** bold wolf (Germanic).

**Wolfram** wolf raven (Germanic).

**Woodrow** a surname, meaning row (of houses) in a wood, used as a first name; a diminutive form is *Woody*.

**Woody** a diminutive form of Woodrow, now used independently.

**Wordsworth** a variant form of Wadsworth.

**Wyman** a surname, meaning battle protector, used as a first name (Old English).

**Wyn** white (Welsh); a variant form is Wynn.

**Wyndham** a surname, meaning homestead of Wyman, used as a first name (Old English); a variant form is *Windham*.

**Wynn, Wynne** a surname, meaning friend, used as a first name; a variant form of Wyn.

**Xavier** a placename, meaning new house owner, used as a first name (Spanish/Basque).

**Xenos** stranger (Greek).
**Xerxes** royal (Persian).

**Y**

**Yale** a surname, meaning fertile upland (Welsh).
**Yamir** moon (Indian).
**Yasaar** wealth (Indian).
**Yash** success (Indian).
**Yashas** fame (Indian).
**Yasir** wealthy (Indian).
**Yatin** devotee (Indian).
**Yehudi** a Jew (Hebrew).
**Yogi** devotee (Indian).
**Yoonus** a Prophet's name (Indian).
**Yoosuf** a Prophet's name (Indian).
**Yudhishthir** eldest Pandava brother (Indian).
**Yuri** a Russian form of George.
**Yuvraj** a prince (Indian).
**Yves** yew tree (French-Germanic).

**Z**

**Zaafir** victorious (Indian).
**Zaahid** abstemious (Indian).
**Zaahir** bright; shining (Indian).

**Zabdiel** gift of God (Hebrew).
**Zaccheus** innocent; pure (Hebrew).
**Zachary, Zachariah, Zacharias, Zecheriah** Jehovah has remembered (Hebrew); diminutive forms are *Zach, Zack, Zak.*
**Zadok** righteous (Hebrew).
**Zakariya** a Prophet's name (Indian).
**Zakiy** pure (Indian).
**Zebadiah, Zebedee** gift of the Lord (Hebrew).
**Zebulon, Zebulun** elevation (Hebrew); diminutive forms are *Lonny, Zeb.*
**Zedekiah** justice of the Lord (Hebrew); a diminutive form is *Zed.*
**Zeke** a diminutive form of Ezekiel.
**Zelig** a variant form of Selig.
**Zenas** gift of Zeus (Greek).
**Zephaniah** hid of the Lord (Hebrew); a diminutive form is *Zeph.*

**Aalia** exalted; highest social standing (Indian).

**Abbie, Abby** diminutive forms of Abigail, also used independently.

**Abeer** fragrance (Indian).

**Aberah** a variant form of Averah.

**Abhilasha** wish, desire (Indian).

**Abigail** my father's joy (Hebrew); diminutive forms are *Abbie, Abby, Gail.*

**Abra** mother of multitudes (Hebrew).

**Acacia** the name of a plant, possibly meaning immortality and resurrection, used as a first name (Greek).

**Acantha** thorny, spiny (Greek).

**Ada** diminutive of Adela or names beginning with Adal, also used independently; a variant form of Adah.

**Adabelle** joyful and beautiful, a combination of Ada and Belle; variant forms are *Adabel, Adabela, Adabella.*

**Adah** ornament (Hebrew); a variant form is *Ada.*

**Adalia** an early Saxon tribal name whose origin is unknown (Germanic).

**Adamina** fem of Adam (Latin).

**Adar** fire; as the name in the Jewish calendar for the twelfth month of the Biblical year and the sixth month of the civil year, it is a name sometimes given to girls born in that period (Hebrew).

**Adeela** equal (Indian).

**Adela** of noble birth; a princess (Germanic).

**Adelaide** of noble birth; a princess (Germanic); a diminutive form is *Addie.*

**Adèle, Adele** the French form of Adela, now also used as an English form.

**Adelheid** noble kind (Germanic); a diminutive form is *Heidi.*

**Adeline, Adelina** of noble birth; a princess (Germanic); a diminutive form is *Aline.*

**Adelphia** sisterly, eternal friend of mankind (Greek); variant forms are *Adelfia, Adelpha.*

**Adina** voluptuous, ripe, mature (Hebrew).

**Adrianne, Adrienne** fem forms of Adrian.

**Africa** the name of the continent used as a first name.

**Agatha** good; kind (Greek); a diminutive form is *Aggie, Aggy*.

**Agave** illustrious, famous (Greek).

**Agnes** chaste; pure (Greek); diminutive forms are *Aggie, Aggy, Agneta, Nessa, Nessie*.

**Aida** visiting, returning (Indian).

**Ailean** Scots Gaelic form of Alan.

**Aileen** a variant form of Eileen.

**Ailsa** fairy (Scots Gaelic).

**Aimée** the French form of Amy.

**Áine** an Irish Gaelic form of Anna.

**Aisleen, Aisling** vision (Irish Gaelic).

**Alana, Alanna, Alannah** fem of Alan; a variant form is *Lana*.

**Alberta** fem form of Albert.

**Alda** wise and rich (Germanic); variant forms are *Eada, Elda*.

**Aldora** of noble rank (Old English); variant forms are *Aelda, Aeldra*.

**Aleria** like an eagle (Latin).

**Alethea** truth (Greek).

**Alexandra, Alexandrina** fem forms of Alexander; diminutives are *Alex, Alexa, Lexie, Lexy, Sandie, Sandra, Sandy*.

**Alexia** fem form of Alexis.

**Alexina** fem form of Alexander.

**Alfonsine** fem form of Alphonse (Germanic); variant forms are *Alphonsina, Alphonsine, Alphonza*.

**Alfreda** fem form of Alfred; diminutive forms are *Alfie, Allie; variant forms are Elfreda, Elfreida, Elfrieda, Elfrida, Elva, Elga, Freda*.

**Alia** exalted, highest social standing (Indian).

**Alice, Alicia** of noble birth; a princess (Germanic); variant forms are *Alys, Alyssa*.

**Alida** little bird; small and lithe (Latin); a Hungarian form of Adelaide; variant forms are *Aleda, Aleta, Alita*; diminutive forms are *Leda, Lita*.

**Aliénor** a French form of Eleanor.

**Alima** learned in music and dancing (Arabic).

**Aline** a contraction of Adeline.

**Alisha** protected (Indian).

**Alison** diminutive of Alice, now

used entirely in its own right; a variant form is *Allison*; diminutive forms are *Allie, Ally*.

**Alix** a variant form of Alex.

**Allegra** a word for cheerful or blithe used as a first name (Italian).

**Alma** loving, nurturing (Latin).

**Almira** lofty; a princess (Arabic).

**Aloha** a word for welcome used as a first name (Hawaiian).

**Alpana** beautiful (Indian).

**Alta** tall in spirit (Latin).

**Althea** a healer (Greek); a diminutive form is *Thea*.

**Alura** divine counsellor (Old English).

**Alva** white (Latin).

**Alvina, Alvine** beloved and noble friend (Germanic); a diminutive form is *Vina*.

**Amalia** work (Germanic); an Italian and Greek form of Amelia.

**Amanda** worthy of love (Latin); diminutive forms are *Manda, Mandy*.

**Amber** the name of a gemstone used as a first name.

**Amelia** busy, energetic (Germanic); a diminutive form is *Millie*.

**Amélie** the French form of Amelia.

**Amelinda** beloved and pretty (Spanish); variant forms are *Amalinda, Amelinde*.

**Amena** honest, truthful (Gaelic).

**Ameena** trustworthy; faithful (Indian).

**Ameera** leader, princess (Indian).

**Amethyst** the name of the semi-precious gemstone used as a first name (Greek).

**Aminta, Amintha, Aminthe** protector, a shepherdess in Greek mythology (Greek).

**Amy** beloved (Old French).

**Anahita** full of grace (Indian).

**Anastasia** rising up, resurrection (Greek); diminutive forms are *Stacey, Stacy, Stacie, Stasia*.

**Anatholia, Anatola** fem forms of Anatole (Greek); a variant form is *Anatolia*.

**Andrea** fem form of Andreas or Andrew; a variant form is *Andrina*.

**Aneesa** friendly (Indian).

**Anemone** windflower, the name of the garden plant used as a first name (Greek).

**Angela, Angelina** messenger (Greek); diminutive forms are *Angel* and *Angie*.

**Angelica** lovely; angelic (Greek).

**Angharad** much loved (Welsh).

**Anisha** unobstructed (Indian).

**Anita** Spanish diminutive of Ann, now used independently as an English-language form; a diminutive form is *Nita*.

**Anjali** offering (Hindu).

**Ann** grace (Hebrew); a variant form is *Hannah*; a diminutive form is *Annie*.

**Anna** the Latin form of Ann.

**Annabel, Annabelle, Annabella** lovable (possibly from Amabel); diminutive forms are *Bella, Belle*.

**Anne** the French form of Ann.

**Anneka** a Dutch diminutive of Anna.

**Annette** a French diminutive of Ann, used as an English-language form.

**Annika** a Swedish diminutive of Anna.

**Annis, Annice** a medieval diminutive of Agnes.

**Annunciata** Italian form of nuntius, bringer of news, i.e. the angel Gabriel, who delivered the announcement of the Virgin Mary's conception, a name often given to children born on 25 March, Lady Day (Latin).

**Anona** annual crops, hence the Roman goddess of crops (Latin); a variant form is *Annona*; diminutives are *Nonnie, Nona*.

**Anora** light, graceful (Old English).

**Anselma** fem form of Anselm; a variant form is *Arselma*.

**Anshula** sunny (Indian).

**Anthea** flowery (Greek).

**Antoinette** diminutive of Antonia, now used as an English-language form; a diminutive form is *Toni*.

**Antonia** fem form of Antony; diminutive forms are *Toni, Tonia, Tonie, Tony*.

**Anuradha** a bright star (Hindu).

**Anushka** a term of endearment (Indian).

**April** the name of the month, Aprilis, used as a personal name (Latin).

**Ara** spirit of revenge, and the goddess of destruction and vengeance (Greek).

**Arabella, Arabela** a fair altar (Latin); a woman (Arabic); diminutive forms are *Bella, Belle*.

**Araminta** beautiful, sweet-smelling flower (Greek); a diminutive form is *Minta*.

**Ariadne** very holy (Greek).

**Arianna** an Italian form of Ariadne.

**Ariella, Arielle** fem forms of Ariel (Hebrew).

**Arlene** fem form of Arlen; a variant form of Charlene, Marlene; variant forms are *Arleen, Arlena, Arlina, Arline, Arlyne*.

**Armelle** fem form of Armel.

**Armilla** bracelet (Latin).

**Armina, Armine** fem forms of Armin; variant forms are *Erminie, Erminia*.

**Arnalda** fem form of Arnold (Germanic).

**Artemis** the name of the virgin Greek goddess of hunting and the moon, the derivation of which is unknown. The Roman equivalent is Diana.

**Arva** ploughed land, pasture (Latin).

**Arwenna** fem form of Arwyn.

**Astrid** fair god (Norse); a diminutive is *Astra*.

**Atalanta, Atalante** the name of a mythological character who agreed to marry the man who could outrun her (Greek); a variant form is *Atlanta*.

**Atalya** guardian (Spanish).

**Athena, Athene, Athenée** in Greek mythology, the goddess of wisdom. Her Roman counterpart is Minerva (Greek).

**Atif** generous (Indian).

**Atula** uncomparable (Indian).

**Audrey** noble might (Old English).

**Augusta** fem form of Augustus; diminutive forms are *Gussie, Gusta*.

**Aura, Aure, Aurea** breath of air (Latin); a variant form is *Auria*.

**Aurelia** fem form of Aurelius.

**Aurora** morning redness; fresh; brilliant (Latin).

**Autumn** the name of the season, the origin of which is uncertain, used as a first name.

**Ava** origin uncertain, perhaps a Germanic diminutive of names beginning Av-.

**Avera** transgressor (Hebrew); a variant form is *Aberah*.

**Averil, Averill** English forms of Avril.

**Avice, Avis** possibly bird (Latin).

**Avril** the French form of April.

**Ayesha** the name of the

favourite wife of the Prophet Mohammad.

**Azaliea, Azalia, Azalee** variant forms of the name of the azalea plant, supposed to prefer dry earth, used as a first name.

**Azura, Azure** blue as the sky (French).

**Azza** young female gazelle (Indian).

# B

**Baasima** smiling (Indian).

**Balqis** the name of the Queen of Sheba (Indian).

**Bambi** a variant form of the word for bambino, child (Italian).

**Baptista** fem form of Baptist.

**Barbara, Barbra** foreign, strange (Greek); diminutive forms are *Bab, Babs, Barbie*.

**Basanti** spring (Indian).

**Basheera** bringer of good tidings (Indian).

**Basilia** fem form of Basil.

**Bathilda** battle commander (Germanic).

**Bathsheba** daughter of plenty (Hebrew).

**Beata** blessed, divine one (Latin); a diminutive form is *Bea*.

**Beatrice, Beatrix** woman who blesses (Latin); diminutive forms are *Bea, Beatie, Beaty, Bee, Trix, Trixie*.

**Beckie, Becky** diminutive forms of Rebecca.

**Beda** maid of war (Old English).

**Belinda** a name used by Sir John Vanburgh in his play The Provok'd Wife, its origin is uncertain, possibly beautiful woman (Italian).

**Beena** a musical instrument (Indian).

**Bella, Belle** beautiful (French, Italian); diminutive forms of Annabel, Arabella, Isabella.

**Bena** wise one (Hebrew).

**Benedicta** fem form of Benedict; a contracted form is *Benita*; a diminutive form is *Dixie*.

**Benita** fem form of Benito; a contracted form of Benedicta.

**Berenice** bringing victory (Greek); also *Bernice*.

**Bernadette** fem form of Bernard.

**Berta** a German, Italian and Spanish form of Bertha.

**Beryl** jewel (Greek), the name of the gemstone used as a first name.

**Bess, Bessie** diminutive forms of Elizabeth.

**Beth** a diminutive form of Elizabeth, Bethany, now used independently.

**Bethan** a Welsh diminutive form of Elizabeth-Ann also used independently.

**Bethany** a placename near Jerusalem, the home of Lazarus in the New Testament and meaning house of poverty, used as a first name (Aramaic).

**Betsy, Bette, Bettina, Betty** diminutive forms of Elizabeth.

**Beulah** married (Hebrew).

**Bhadra** good (Indian).

**Bhanuni** charming woman (Indian).

**Bhavi** emotional (Indian).

**Bhuvi** heaven (Indian).

**Bianca** the Italian form of Blanche, now also used independently as an English-language form.

**Biddy** a diminutive form of Bridget.

**Birgit** the Swedish form of *Bridget*; a diminutive form is *Britt*.

**Bishakha** star (Indian).

**Blanca** the Spanish form of Blanche.

**Blanche** white (Germanic).

**Blodwen** white flower (Welsh).

**Blossom** like a flower (Old English).

**Bonita** pretty (Spanish); good (Latin); a diminutive form is *Bonnie*.

**Bonnie** pretty (Scots English); a diminutive form of Bonita.

**Branwen** raven-haired beauty (Welsh); a variant form of Bronwen.

**Brenda** a brand or sword (Old Norse).

**Brenna** raven-haired beauty (Irish Gaelic).

**Bridget** goddess of fire (Celtic); a variant form is *Brigid*; diminutive forms are *Biddy*, *Bridie*.

**Briony** a variant form of Bryony.

**Britt** a diminutive form of Birgit, now used independently.

**Brittany** the anglicized name of a French region, meaning land of the figured, or tattooed folk, used as a first name.

**Bronwen** white breast (Welsh); variant forms are *Bronwyn*, *Branwen*.

**Brook, Brooke** a surname,

meaning stream, used as a first name; a variant form is *Brooks*.

**Brunella** form of Bruno.

**Brunhilda, Brunhilde** warrior maid (Germanic).

**Brynmor** large hill (Welsh).

**Bryony** the name of a climbing plant used as a first name (Greek); a variant form is Briony.

**Buena** good (Spanish).

**Bunty** a diminutive meaning lamb, now used as a first name (English).

**Buona** good (Italian).

**Bushra** good omen (Indian).

# C

**Cadence** rhythmic (Latin).

**Cadenza** the Italian form of Cadence.

**Cáit** the Irish Gaelic form of Kate.

**Caitlín, Caitrín** Irish Gaelic forms of Katherine.

**Calandra** lark (Greek);

diminutive forms are *Cal, Callie, Cally*.

**Calandre** the French form of Calandra.

**Calandria** the Spanish form of Calandra.

**Calantha** beautiful blossom (Greek); diminutive forms are *Cal, Callie, Cally*.

**Calanthe** the French form of Calantha.

**Caledonia** the Roman name for Scotland used as a first name (Latin).

**Calla** beautiful (Greek).

**Calliope** lovely voice; the muse of poetry (Greek).

**Callista** fem form of Callisto.

**Calumina** fem form of Calum.

**Calvina** fem form of Calvin.

**Calypso** concealer; in Greek mythology, the sea nymph who held Odysseus captive for seven years (Greek); a variant form is *Kalypso*.

**Camilla** votaress, attendant at a sacrifice (Latin).

**Camille** the French form of Camilla.

**Candice, Candace** meaning uncertain, possibly brilliantly white or pure and virtuous, the name of an Ethiopian queen

(Latin); diminutive forms are *Candie, Candy*.

**Candida** shining white (Latin); diminutive forms are *Candie, Candy*.

**Candy** a diminutive form of Candice, Candida; a name used in its own right, from candy, the American-English word for a sweet.

**Cara** friend (Irish Gaelic); dear, darling (Italian); a variant form is *Carina*.

**Caridad** the Spanish form of Charity.

**Carissa** dear one (Latin).

**Carla** fem form of Carl; a variant form is *Carlin*; diminutive forms are *Carlie, Carley, Carly*.

**Carlotta** the Italian form of Charlotte.

**Carly** a diminutive form of Carla, Carlin, now used independently.

**Carmel** garden (Hebrew).

**Carmela** a Spanish and Italian form of Carmel.

**Carmelita** a Spanish diminutive form of Carmel.

**Carmen** a Spanish form of Carmel.

**Carnation** the name of a flower, meaning flesh colour, sometimes used as a first name (Latin/French).

**Carola** a variant form of Caroline; diminutive forms are *Carrie, Caro, Caddie*.

**Carole** the French form of Carol; a contracted form of Caroline; diminutive forms are *Caro, Carrie, Caddie*.

**Carolina** the Italian and Spanish forms of Caroline.

**Caroline, Carolyn** form of Carolus, the Latin form of Charles; diminutive forms are *Caro, Carrie, Caddie*.

**Carrie** a diminutive form of Carol, Carola, Carole, Caroline, Carolyn.

**Carys** love (Welsh).

**Cassandra** she who inflames with love (Greek); in Greek mythology, a princess whose prophecies of doom were not believed; diminutive forms are *Cass, Cassie*.

**Catalina** the Spanish form of Katherine.

**Caterina** the Italian form of Katherine.

**Catharina, Catharine, Catherina** variant forms of Catherine.

**Catherine** the French form of Katherine, now used as an

English-language form; diminutive forms are *Cath, Cathie, Cathy*.

**Catrin** the Welsh form of Katherine.

**Catriona** the Scots Gaelic form of Katherine.

**Cecile** the French form of Cecily, Cecilia.

**Cecily, Cecilia** fem forms of Cecil; diminutive forms are *Celia, Cis, Cissie, Cissy*; a variant form is *Cicely*.

**Celandine** the name of either of two unrelated flowering plants, meaning swallow, used as a first name (Greek).

**Celeste, Celestine** heavenly (Latin).

**Celia** heavenly (Latin); diminutive form of Cecilia.

**Cendrillon** from the ashes, the fairytale heroine (French); the anglicized form is *Cinderella*.

**Cerian** diminutive form of Ceri.

**Cerys** love (Welsh).

**Chahna** love (Indian).

**Chameli** a flower (Indian).

**Chandani** moonlight (Indian).

**Chandi** great goddess (Indian).

**Chandra** moon brighter than the stars (Sanskrit).

**Chanel** the surname of the French couturier and perfumier, Coco Chanel, used as a first name.

**Charis** grace (Greek).

**Charita** good (Indian).

**Charity** the abstract noun for the quality of tolerance or generosity used as a personal name (Old French).

**Charlene** a relatively modern diminutive form of Charles.

**Charlotte** fem form of Charles (Germanic); diminutive forms are *Charlie, Charley, Lottie*.

**Charmaine** a diminutive form of the abstract noun for the quality of pleasing or attracting people used as a first name; a variant form of Charmian.

**Charmian** little delight (Greek); a modern variant form is *Charmaine*.

**Charu** beautiful (Indian).

**Charusheela** beautiful jewel (Indian).

**Chelsea** a placename, meaning chalk landing place, sometimes used as a first name (Old English).

**Cher, Chérie** dear, darling (French).

**Cherry** the name of the fruit used as a first name; a form of Chérie; a variant form is *Cheryl*.

**Cheryl** a variant form of Cherry; a combining form of Cherry and Beryl; a variant form is *Sheryl*.

**Chloë, Chloe** a green herb; a young shoot (Greek).

**Christian** belonging to Christ; a believer in Christ (Latin); diminutive forms are *Chris, Christie, Christy*.

**Christiana** form of Christian; a variant form is *Christina*.

**Christine** a French form of Christina, now used as an English-language form; diminutive forms are *Chris, Chrissie, Christie, Christy, Teenie, Tina*.

**Ciara** fem form of Ciarán.

**Cicely** a variant form of Cecilia.

**Cilla** a diminutive form of Priscilla (French).

**Cindy** a diminutive form of Cinderella, Cynthia, Lucinda, now often used independently.

**Claire** the French form of Clara, now used widely as an English form.

**Clara** bright, illustrious, renowned (Latin); a variant form is *Clare*; a diminutive form is *Clarrie*.

**Clarabel, Clarabella, Clarabelle** a combination of Clara and Bella or Belle, meaning bright, shining beauty (Latin/French); a variant form is *Claribel*.

**Clarice** fame (Latin); a variant form of Clara; a variant form is *Clarissa*.

**Clementine, Clementina** fem forms of Clement; diminutive forms are *Clem, Clemmie*.

**Cleo** a short form of Cleopatra, used independently.

**Cleopatra** father's glory (Greek); a diminutive form is *Cleo*.

**Cliantha** glory flower (Greek); a diminutive form is *Clia*.

**Clio** glory (Greek).

**Clorinda** a combination of Chloris and Belinda or Lucinda.

**Clothilde, Clotilde** famous fighting woman (Germanic).

**Clover** the name of a flowering plant used as a first name (English).

**Colette** a diminutive form of Nicole, now used independently; a variant form is *Collette*.

**Colleen** the Irish word for a girl, used as a first name.

**Concepcion** beginning, conception, a reference to the

Immaculate Conception of the Virgin Mary (Spanish); diminutive forms are *Concha, Conchita*.

**Constance** fem form of Constant; diminutive forms are *Con, Connie*; a variant form is *Constanta*.

**Consuela** consolation, a reference to the Virgin Mary (Spanish).

**Cora** maiden (Greek).

**Coral** the name of the pink marine jewel material used as a first name.

**Coralie** the French form of Coral.

**Corazón** (sacred) heart (Spanish).

**Cordelia** warm-hearted (Latin).

**Corinna, Corinne** variant forms of Cora.

**Cornelia** fem form of Cornelius.

**Corona** crown (Latin).

**Cosima** fem form of Cosmo.

**Costanza** an Italian form of Constance.

**Courtney** a surname, meaning short nose, used as a first name (Old French).

**Cressida** gold (Greek); a contracted form is *Cressa*.

**Cristina** the Italian, Portuguese and Spanish form of Christina.

**Crystal** the name of a very clear brilliant glass used as a first name; variant forms are *Cristal, Chrystal*.

**Cynthia** belonging to Mount Cynthus (Greek); diminutive forms are *Cindie, Cindy*.

# D

**Dagmar** bright day (Norse).

**Daisy** the name of the plant; the day's eye (Old English).

**Dalaja** honey (Indian).

**Daley** a surname, meaning assembly, used as a first name (Irish Gaelic); a variant form is *Daly*.

**Dalilah, Dalila** variant forms of Delilah.

**Dana** a surname, of uncertain meaning, possibly Danish, used as a first name (Old English).

**Danaë** in Greek mythology, the

mother of Perseus by Zeus, who came to her as a shower of gold while she was in prison; diminutive forms are *Dannie, Danny*.

**Danielle** fem form of Daniel.

**Daphne** laurel (Greek).

**Darcie** a fem form of Darcy.

**Daria** a fem form of Darius.

**Darlene, Darleen** the endearment 'darling' combined with a suffix to form a first name (Old English).

**Davina** fem form of David.

**Daya** compassion (Indian).

**Dawn** the name of the first part of the day derived from the Latin *Aurora* and used as a personal name in the English form.

**Deana, Deane** fem form of Dean; variants forms are *Dena, Dene*.

**Deanna** a variant form of Diana.

**Deborah, Debra** bee (Hebrew); diminutive forms are *Deb, Debbie, Debby*.

**Dee** a diminutive form of names beginning with D.

**Deirdre** meaning uncertain, possibly sorrowful (Irish Gaelic).

**Delia** woman of Delos (Greek).

**Delicia** great delight (Latin).

**Delight** the abstract noun for great pleasure, satisfaction or joy used as a first name (Old French).

**Delilah, Delila** meaning uncertain, possibly delicate (Hebrew); variant forms are *Dalila, Dalilah*; a diminutive form is *Lila*.

**Delma** fem form of Delmar; a diminutive form of Fidelma.

**Delphine** dolphin (Latin); a variant form is *Delfine*.

**Delyth** pretty (Welsh).

**Demetria** fem from Demeter, goddess of the harvest (Greek).

**Denise** fem form of Denis; a variant form is *Denice*.

**Desdemona** ill-fated (Greek), the name given by Shakespeare to the wife of Othello.

**Desirée** longed for (French).

**Devaki** mother of Krishna (Hindu).

**Devangi** like a goddess (Indian).

**Devmani** divine gift (Indian).

**Dhara** earth (Indian).

**Dhriti** patience (Indian).

**Dhwani** melody; music (Indian).

**Dhyana** meditation (Indian).

**Diana** goddess (Latin).

**Diane, Dianne** French forms of Diana.

**Dido** teacher (Greek), in Greek mythology a princess from Tyre who founded Carthage and became its queen.

**Dilys** sure, genuine (Welsh); a diminutive form is *Dilly*.

**Dina** fem form of Dino; a variant form of *Dinah*.

**Dinah** vindicated (Hebrew); a variant form is *Dina*; a diminutive form is *Di*.

**Dione, Dionne** daughter of heaven and earth (Greek), in Greek mythology the earliest consort of Zeus and mother of Aphrodite.

**Dipti** brightness (Indian).

**Divya** heavenly, brilliant (Hindu), divine power (Indian).

**Dixie** a diminutive form of Benedicta.

**Dolina** a Scottish variant form of Donalda.

**Dolly** a diminutive form of Dorothy.

**Dolores** sorrows (Spanish); a variant form is *Delores*; diminutive forms are *Lola, Lolita*.

**Donalda** fem form of Donald.

**Donata** fem form of Donato.

**Donna** lady (Italian).

**Dora** a diminutive form of Dorothea, Theodora, etc., now used independently; diminutive forms are *Dorrie, Dorry*.

**Dorcas** a gazelle (Greek).

**Doreen** an Irish variant form of Dora.

**Dorinda** lovely gift (Greek); diminutive forms are *Dorrie, Dorry*.

**Doris** Dorian woman, one of a Hellenic people who invaded Greece in the 2nd century bc (Greek); diminutive forms are *Dorrie, Dorry*.

**Dorothea** a German form of Dorothy; a diminutive form is *Thea*.

**Dorothy** the gift of God (Greek); diminutive forms are *Dodie, Dodo, Dolly, Dot*.

**Dristi** sight, a form of the Devi (Hindu).

**Drusilla** with dewy eyes (Latin).

**Dulcie** a diminutive form of Dulcibella, meaning sweet beautiful (Latin).

**Dyan** a variant form of Diane.

**Dymphna** little fawn (Irish Gaelic).

**Dyuti** light (Indian).

# E

**Éanna** bird (Irish Gaelic); an anglicized form is Enda.

**Earlene, Earline** fem forms of Earl; variant forms are *Erlene, Erline*; diminutive forms are *Earlie, Earley*.

**Eartha** of the earth (Old English); a variant form is *Ertha*.

**Easter** the name of the Christian festival, used as a first name.

**Ebba** wild boar (Germanic); an Old English form of Eve.

**Ebony** the name of the dark hard wood used as a first name.

**Echo** the name for the physical phenomenon of the reflection of sound or other radiation used as a first name; in Greek mythology it is the name of the nymph who pined away for love of Narcissus.

**Eda** prosperity, happiness (Old English).

**Edana** fem form of Edan.

**Edha** sacred (Indian).

**Edie** a diminutive form of Edina, Edith, Edwina.

**Edina** a Scottish variant form of Edwina.

**Edith** prosperity strife (Old English); variant forms are *Edyth, Edythe*; diminutive forms are *Edie, Edy*.

**Edlyn** noble maid (Old English).

**Edmonda** fem form of Edmund (Old English).

**Edna** pleasure (Hebrew).

**Edrea** fem form of Edric.

**Edwardina** fem form of Edward.

**Edwige** the French form of Hedwig.

**Edwina** fem form of Edwin; a variant form is *Edina*.

**Eesha** purity (Indian).

**Egberta** fem form of Egbert (Old English).

**Eglantine** an alternative name for the wild rose, meaning sharp, keen, used as a first name (Old French).

**Eila** the earth (Indian).

**Eileen** the Irish form of Helen; a variant form is Aileen.

**Eilidh** a Scots Gaelic form of Helen.

**Eirlys** snowdrop (Welsh).

**Eithne** kernel (Irish Gaelic); anglicized forms are *Ena, Ethna*.

73

**Ekaa** Goddess Durga (Indian).

**Ekaja** only child (Indian).

**Ekani** one (Indian).

**Ekanta** devoted girl (Indian).

**Ekantika** singly focused (Indian).

**Ekta** unity (Indian).

**Elaine** a French form of Helen.

**Eldora** a shortened form of El Dorado, meaning the land of gold, used as a first name (Spanish).

**Eldrida** fem form of Eldrid.

**Eleanor, Eleanore** variant forms of Helen; a variant form is *Elinor*; diminutive forms are *Ella, Nell, Nora*.

**Eleanora** the Italian form of Eleanor.

**Electra** brilliant (Greek).

**Elen** angel, nymph (Welsh).

**Elena** the Italian and Spanish form of Helen.

**Elfleda** noble beauty (Old English).

**Elfreda** elf strength (Old English).

**Elga** holy (Old Norse); a variant form of Olga.

**Elin** a Welsh diminutive form of Elinor; a Welsh variant form of Helen.

**Elina** woman with intelligence (Indian).

**Elinor** a variant form of Eleanor.

**Elisa** an Italian diminutive form of Elisabetta.

**Elisabeth** a French and German form of Elizabeth.

**Elisabetta** an Italian form of Elizabeth.

**Élise** a French diminutive form of Elisabeth.

**Elizabeth** worshipper of God; consecrated to God (Hebrew); diminutive forms are *Bess, Bet, Beth, Betsy, Betty, Eliza, Elsa, Elsie, Libby, Lisa, Liza, Lisbeth, Liz*.

**Ella** a diminutive form of Cinderella, Eleanor, Isabella.

**Ellen** a variant form of Helen.

**Ellice** fem form of Elias, Ellis.

**Ellie** a diminutive form of Alice.

**Elma** a diminutive form of Wilhelmina; a contracted form of Elizabeth Mary.

**Elina** woman with intelligence (Indian).

**Éloise, Eloisa** sound, whole (Germanic); a variant form is *Héloïse*.

**Elsa** a diminutive form of Alison, Alice, Elizabeth.

**Elsie** a diminutive form of Alice,

Alison, Elizabeth, Elspeth.

**Elspeth, Elspet** Scottish forms of Elizabeth; diminutive forms are *Elsie, Elspie*.

**Eluned** idol (Welsh).

**Elva** friend of the elf (Old English); a variant form is Elvina.

**Elvira** white (Latin).

**Emeline** a variant form of Amelia; a diminutive form of Emma; a variant form is *Emmeline*.

**Emerald** the name of the green gemstone used as a first name.

**Emilia** the Italian form of Emily.

**Emilie** the German form of Emily.

**Emily** of a noble Roman family the origin of whose name, Aemilius, is uncertain.

**Emma** whole, universal (Germanic); diminutive forms are *Emm, Emmie*.

**Ena** an anglicized form of Eithne.

**Enda** an anglicized form of Éanna.

**Enfys** rainbow (Welsh).

**Engelberta, Engelbertha, Engelberthe** fem forms of Engelbert.

**Enid** meaning uncertain,

possibly woodlark (Welsh).

**Enrica** the Italian form of Henrietta.

**Enrichetta** the Italian form of Henrietta.

**Enriqueta** the Spanish form of Henrietta.

**Eranthe** flower of spring (Greek).

**Erda** of the earth (Germanic).

**Erica** fem form of Eric; a variant form is *Erika*.

**Erin** the poetic name for Ireland, used as a first name.

**Erlene, Erline** variant forms of Earlene, Erline; diminutive forms are *Erlie, Erley*.

**Erma** warrior maid (Germanic).

**Erna** a diminutive form of Ernesta, Ernestine.

**Ernesta** fem form of Ernest; a diminutive form is *Erna*.

**Ernestine** fem form of Ernest; diminutive forms are *Erna, Tina*.

**Esmé** beloved (French).

**Esmeralda** a Spanish form of Emerald.

**Esta** a variant form of Esther.

**Estelle, Estella** variant forms of Stella.

**Esther** the planet Venus (Persian); a variant form is *Esta*;

diminutive forms are *Ess, Essie, Tess, Tessie*.

**Estrella** the Spanish form of Estelle.

**Ethel** noble; of noble birth (Old English).

**Etta, Ettie** diminutive forms of Henrietta.

**Eudora** good gift (Greek).

**Eugenia** fem form of Eugene; diminutive forms are *Ena, Gene*.

**Eugénie** the French form of Eugenia.

**Eulalie** fair speech (Greek).

**Eunice** good victory (Greek).

**Euphemia** of good report (Greek); diminutive forms are *Fay, Effie, Phamie, Phemie*.

**Eustacia** fem form of Eustace; diminutive forms are *Stacey, Stacie, Stacy*.

**Eva** the German, Italian and Spanish forms of Eve.

**Evadne** of uncertain meaning, possibly high-born (Greek).

**Evangeline** good tidings (Greek).

**Eve** life (Hebrew); diminutive forms are *Evie, Evelina, Eveline, Eveleen*.

**Eveline** a diminutive form of Eva, Eve.

**Evelyn** the English surname used as a first name.

**Evita** Spanish diminutive form of Eva.

**Evodia** good journey (Greek).

# F

**Fabia** fem form of Fabio; a variant form is *Fabiola*.

**Fabienne** fem form of Fabien.

**Faith** the quality of belief or fidelity, used as a first name.

**Fanny** a diminutive form of Frances, also used independently.

**Fatima** the name of the daughter of Mohammed (Semitic); of Fatima in Portugal (Portuguese).

**Faustina, Faustine** lucky (Latin).

**Fawn** the name for a young deer or a light greyish-brown colour used as a first name (Old French).

**Fay, Faye** faith or fairy (Old French); a diminutive form of Euphemia.

**Felicia** fem form of Felix.

**Felicidad** the Spanish form of Felicia.

**Felicity** happiness (Latin).

**Fenella** an anglicized form of Fionnuala.

**Fern** the name of the plant, sometimes used as a first name (Old English).

**Fernanda** fem form of Ferdinand.

**Ffion** foxglove (Welsh).

**Fidelia** a variant form of Fidelis; a diminutive form is *Fid*.

**Fidelis** faithful (Latin); a variant form is *Fidelia*; a diminutive form is *Fid*.

**Fidelma** faithful Mary (Latin/Irish Gaelic); a diminutive form is *Delma*.

**Fifi** a French diminutive form of Josephine.

**Filippa** the Italian form of Philippa.

**Finola** a variant form of Fionnuala.

**Fiona** white, fair (Scots Gaelic).

**Fionnuala** white shoulder (Irish Gaelic); a diminutive form is *Nuala*, also used independently.

**Fleur** a flower (French).

**Fleurette** little flower (French).

**Flora** flowers; the Roman goddess of flowers (Latin); diminutive forms are *Flo, Florrie, Flossie*.

**Florence** blooming; flourishing (Latin); diminutive forms are *Flo, Florrie, Flossie, Floy*.

**Flower** the English word for a bloom or blossom used as a first name.

**Foram** fragrance (Indian).

**Fortune** the word for wealth, fate or chance used as a first name (Latin); a variant form is *Fortuna*.

**Frances** fem form of Francis; diminutive forms are *Fanny, Fran*.

**Francesca** the Italian form of Frances; a diminutive form is *Francheschina*.

**Francine** a diminutive form of Frances, Françoise.

**Francisca** the Spanish form of Frances.

**Françoise** the French form of Frances.

**Freda** a diminutive form of Winifred; a variant form of Frieda.

**Frederica** fem form of Frederick; diminutive forms are *Fred, Freddie, Freddy, Frieda*.

**Freya** lady, the Norse goddess of love.

**Frieda** peace (Germanic); a diminutive form of Frederica.

**Friederike** the German form of Frederica; a diminutive form is *Fritzi*.

**Fulki** spark (Indian).

**Fulmala** garland (Indian).

**Fulvia** yellow-haired (Latin).

# G

**Gabrielle** fem form of Gabriel; diminutive forms are *Gabbie, Gabby*.

**Gaea** the Latin form of Gaia.

**Gaia** earth, in classical mythology the goddess of the earth (Greek); the Latin form is Gaea.

**Gail** a diminutive form of Abigail, now used independently; variant forms are *Gale, Gayle*.

**Gajra** flowers (Indian).

**Galatea** white as milk, in Greek mythology a statue brought to life (Greek).

**Galia** wave (Hebrew).

**Gandhali** sweet scent (Indian).

**Gardenia** the name of a flowering plant with fragrant flowers, called after Dr Alexander Garden, used as a first name (New Latin).

**Gargi** wise woman (Indian).

**Garima** warmth (Indian).

**Garland** the name for a wreath or crown of flowers used as a first name (Old French).

**Garnet** the name of a deep-red gemstone used as a first name (Old French).

**Gay** the quality of being joyous used as a first name.

**Gayatri** mother of the Vedas (Hindu).

**Gaynor** a medieval English form of Guinevere.

**Gazella** like a gazelle or antelope (Latin).

**Geeta** holy book of the Hindus (Indian).

**Gemma** a gem (Italian); a variant form is *Jemma*.

**Geneva** a variant form of Genevieve; the name of a Swiss city used as a first name.

**Genevieve** meaning uncertain, possibly tribe woman (Celtic).

**Georgia, Georgiana, Georgina** forms of George; a diminutive form is *Georgie*.

**Geraldine** fem form of Gerald.

**Germaine** fem form of Germain; a variant form is *Jermaine*.

**Gertrude** spear maiden (Germanic); diminutive forms are *Gert, Gertie, Trudi, Trudy*.

**Ghaaliya** fragrant (Indian).

**Gigi** a French diminutive form of Georgine, Virginie.

**Gilberta, Gilberte** fem forms of Gilbert; diminutive forms are *Gill, Gillie, Gilly*.

**Gilda** sacrifice (Germanic).

**Gillian** fem form of Julian; diminutive forms are *Gill, Gillie, Gilly*.

**Gina** a diminutive form of Georgina, also used independently.

**Ginni** precious gold coin (Indian).

**Ginnie, Ginny** a diminutive form of Virginia.

**Giovanna** the Italian form of Jane.

**Girisha** goddess Parvati (Indian).

**Giselle** promise, pledge (Germanic).

**Gitana** gipsy (Spanish).

**Gladys** the anglicized Welsh form of Claudia.

**Glenda** clean and good (Welsh); a variant form is *Glenys*.

**Glenna** fem form of Glen.

**Gloria** glory (Latin).

**Glynis** fem form of Glyn; a variant form of Glenys.

**Godavri** a river (Indian).

**Godiva** gift of God (Old English).

**Golda, Golde** gold (Yiddish).

**Goldie** an anglicized form of Golda; fair-haired (English).

**Grace** grace (Latin); a diminutive form is *Gracie*.

**Gráinne** loved (Irish Gaelic). A variant form is *Grania*.

**Greta** a diminutive form of Margaret.

**Gretchen** a diminutive form of Margaret, Margarete.

**Grete** a diminutive form of Margarete.

**Griselda, Grizelda** stone heroine (Germanic); diminutive forms are *Grissel, Grizel, Grizzel*.

**Gudrun** God's secret (Old Norse).

**Guinevere** white and soft, the name of the wife of King Arthur (Welsh).

**Gulab** a rose (Indian).

**Gunhilda, Gunhilde** warrior maid (Old Norse).

**Gunnika** garland (Indian).

**Gussie, Gusta** diminutive forms of Augusta.

**Gwenda** a diminutive form of Gwendolen, also used independently.

**Gwendolen, Gwendolin, Gwendolyn** white ring or bow (Welsh); diminutive forms are *Gwen, Gwenda, Gwennie*.

**Gwyneth** blessed (Welsh).

**Gypsy** the name for a member of a people who live a nomadic life, used as a first name; a variant form is *Gipsy*.

# H

**Hadiya** a gift (Indian).

**Hagar** flight (Hebrew).

**Haidee** modest, honoured (Greek); a variant form of Heidi.

**Halcyon, Halcyone** variant forms of Alcyone.

**Haldan, Haldane, Halden, Haldin** a surname, meaning half Dane, used as a surname (Old English).

**Haimi** golden (Indian).

**Haleema** gentle; patient (Indian).

**Hana** happiness (Indian).

**Haniya** pleased, happy (Indian).

**Hannah** grace (Hebrew); a variant form is *Ann*; a diminutive form is *Nana*.

**Happy** an English adjective, meaning feeling, showing or expressing joy, now used as a first name (Old English).

**Haralda** fem form of Harold.

**Haribala** daughter of Lord Vishnu (Indian).

**Harmony** the word for the quality of concord used as a first name (Greek).

**Harriet, Harriot** fem forms of Harry; diminutive forms are *Hattie, Hatty*.

**Harshita** one who brings happiness (Indian).

**Hasita** full of laughter (Indian).

**Hasna** beautiful (Indian).

**Hayley** a surname, meaning hay clearing, used as a first

name (Old English); a variant form is *Haley*.

**Hazel** the name of a tree used as a first name (Old English).

**Heather** the name of a purple or white-flowered plant of the heath family used as a first name (Old English).

**Hebe** young (Greek). In Greek mythology, the daughter of Zeus and goddess of youth and spring.

**Hedda** war, strife (Germanic).

**Hedwig, Hedvig** strife (Germanic).

**Heidi** diminutive of Adelheid; a variant form is *Haidee*.

**Helen, Helena** light (Greek); diminutive forms are *Nell, Lena*.

**Helga** healthy, happy, holy (Old Norse).

**Helma** protection (Germanic).

**Héloïse** a French variant form of *Éloïse*.

**Hemakshi** golden eyes (Indian).

**Henrietta** fem form of Henry; diminutive forms are *Hettie, Hetty, Netta, Nettie*.

**Henriette** the French form of Henrietta.

**Hephzibah** my delight is in her (Hebrew); a diminutive form is *Hepsy*.

**Hera** queen of heaven; in Greek mythology, the sister and wife of Zeus (Greek). Her counterpart in Roman mythology is Juno.

**Hermione** a name derived from that of Hermes.

**Hermosa** beautiful (Spanish).

**Herta** of the earth (Old English); a variant form is *Hertha*.

**Hessa** destiny (Indian).

**Hester, Hesther** variant forms of Esther.

**Heulwen** sunshine (Welsh).

**Hibernia** the Latin name for Ireland used as a first name.

**Hibiscus** marsh mallow, the name of a brightly flowering plant used as a first name (Greek/Latin).

**Hilary, Hillary** cheerful; merry (Latin).

**Hilda** battle maid (Germanic); a variant form is *Hylda*.

**Hildegarde** strong in battle (Germanic).

**Hiral** wealthy (Indian).

**Holly, Hollie** the name of the red-berried tree used as a first name (English).

**Honey** the word for a sweet substance used as a term of endearment and as a first name.

**Honor, Honora** variant forms of Honour.

**Honoria** honourable (Latin); diminutive forms are *Nora, Norah, Noreen*.

**Honour** the word for personal integrity used as a first name; variant forms are *Honor, Honora*.

**Hope** the word for the feeling of expectation used as a first name (English).

**Horatia** fem form of Horace.

**Hortensia, Hortense** of the garden (Latin).

**Huberta** fem form of Hubert.

**Hulda, Huldah** weasel (Hebrew).

**Hyacinth** the name of the flower adapted from the name of the hero of Greek mythology whose blood, after his killing by Apollo, caused a flower to spring up.

**Hypatia** highest (Greek).

# I

**Ianthe** violet flower (Greek).

**Ida** god-like (Germanic).

**Idabell** god-like and fair.

**Idha** insight (Indian).

**Iditri** complimentary (Indian).

**Idonia** sufficient (Latin).

**Idony, Idonie** in Norse mythology, the keeper of the golden apples of youth (Norse).

**Ignatia** fem form of Ignatius.

**Ikraam** honour (Indian).

**Ilhaam** intuition (Indian).

**Ilona** a Hungarian form of Helen; a diminutive form is *Ilka*.

**Ilse** a diminutive form of Elisabeth.

**Iman** faith (Indian).

**Imogen** from innogen, girl, maiden (Celtic), used by Shakespeare for one of his characters in Cymbeline and misspelled by him or his printer.

**Imperial** relating to an emperor (Latin).

**Inas** capable (Indian).

**India** the name of the country used as a first name.

**Indira** bestower of wealth (Indian).

**Induja** daughter of the moon (Indian).

**Inés, Inez** Spanish forms of Agnes.

**Inga** a diminutive form of Ingeborg, Ingrid.

**Ingeborg** fortification of Ing, the god of fertility (Frey) (Old Norse); diminutive forms are *Inga, Inge*.

**Inger** a variant form of Ingrid.

**Ingrid** maiden of Ing, the god of fertility (Frey) (Old Norse); a variant form is *Inger*; diminutive forms are *Inga, Inge*.

**Innes** island (Scots Gaelic).

**Iola** a variant form of Iole.

**Iolanthe** violet flower (Greek).

**Iole** violet (Greek); a variant form is *Iola*.

**Iona** yew tree (Celtic), the name of the Scottish Hebridean island, used as a first name.

**Ione** a violet (Greek).

**Iphigenia** strong (Greek).

**Ipsita** desire (Indian).

**Irene** peace (Greek); a

diminutive form is *Renie*.

**Iris** rainbow (Greek).

**Irma** noble one (Germanic).

**Isabel, Isabella** Spanish forms of Elizabeth, now used as separate English-language names; variant forms are *Isobel, Ishbel* (particularly in Scotland); diminutive forms are *Ibby, Isa, Izzie, Izzy, Tib, Tibbie*.

**Isabelle** the French form of Isabel.

**Isadora** a variant form of Isidora.

**Iseabail, Ishbel** Scots forms of Isabel.

**Iseult** a French and Welsh form of Isolde.

**Ishya** spring (Indian).

**Isidora** fem form of Isidore; a variant form is *Isadora*.

**Isla, Islay** a Scottish island name, used as a first name.

**Isola** isolated, alone (Latin).

**Isolde, Isolda, Isold** beautiful aspect (Welsh).

**Ita, Ite** thirst (for truth) (Irish Gaelic).

**Ivana** fem form of Ivan.

**Ivy** the name of the plant, used as a first name (Old English).

# J

**Jacinta** the Spanish form of Hyacinth.

**Jacinth** a variant form of Hyacinth.

**Jacoba** fem form of Jacob.

**Jacqueline** fem form of Jacques; a variant form is *Jaqueline*; a diminutive form is *Jackie*.

**Jacquetta** fem form of James.

**Jade** the name of the light-green semi-precious stone, used as a first name.

**Jael** wild she-goat (Hebrew).

**Jalaja** goddess of wealth (Indian).

**Jameerah** beautiful one (Indian).

**Jamesina** fem form of James; a diminutive form is *Ina*.

**Janaan** heart or soul (Indian).

**Jancis** a combination of Jan and Frances; a diminutive form is *Jan*.

**Jane** fem form of John; variant forms are *Janet, Janeta, Janette, Janice, Janine, Jayne, Jean, Joan;* diminutive forms are *Jan, Janey, Janie*.

**Janice** a variant form of Jane.

**Janine** a variant form of Janey.

**Janya** life (Indian).

**Jasmine, Jasmin** the name of the flower, used as a first name; variant forms are *Jessamine, Jessamyn, Yasmin, Yasmine*.

**Jasweer** victorious (Indian).

**Jaya** victory (Hindu).

**Jayani** a sakti of Ganesha (Hindu).

**Jayashree** victorious woman (Indian).

**Jean** a variant form of Jane; a diminutive form is *Jeanie*.

**Jeanette, Jeannette** a diminutive form of Jeanne, now used independently as an English-language name.

**Jeanne** the French form of Jane; a diminutive form is *Jeanette*.

**Jehuda** fem form of Jehudi; a variant form is *Yehuda*.

**Jemima, Jemimah** dove (Hebrew); diminutive forms are *Mima, Mina*.

**Jemma** a variant form of Gemma.

**Jenna, Jenni, Jennie**

diminutive forms of Jane, Jennifer, now used independently; a variant form is *Jenny*.

**Jennifer, Jenifer** the Cornish form of Guinevere; diminutive forms are *Jen, Jennie, Jenny*.

**Jeremia** fem form of Jeremiah.

**Jermaine** a variant form of Germaine.

**Jerusha** possessed; married (Hebrew).

**Jess** a diminutive form of Jessica, Jessie.

**Jessica** God is looking (Hebrew); a diminutive form is *Jess*.

**Jewel** the name for a precious stone or valuable ornament used as a first name.

**Jezebel** domination (Hebrew).

**Jigisha** superior (Indian).

**Jill** a diminutive form of Gillian, Jillian, now used independently.

**Jillian** fem form of Julian; diminutive forms are *Jill, Jilly*.

**Joan, Joann, Joanna, Joanne** forms of John; diminutive forms are *Joanie, Joni*.

**Jobina** fem form of Job.

**Jocelyn, Jocelin** little Goth (Germanic); diminutive forms are *Jos, Joss*.

**Jodie, Jody** diminutive forms of Judith, now used independently.

**Johanna** the Latin and German form of Jane.

**Jolie** from the French meaning pretty, sometimes used as a first name.

**Joni** a diminutive form of Joan.

**Jordana** fem form of Jordan.

**Josceline** fem form of Jocelyn.

**Josefa** fem form of Josef.

**Josephine** fem form of Joseph; diminutive forms are *Jo, Josie, Phenie*.

**Josette** a French diminutive form of Josephine, now used independently.

**Joshika** young maiden (Indian).

**Josie** a diminutive form of Josephine.

**Joy** the name of the feeling of intense happiness used as a first name (English).

**Joyce** sportive (Latin).

**Juana** the Spanish form of Jane; a diminutive form is *Juanita*.

**Judie, Judi** diminutive forms of Judith, now used independently.

**Judith** of Judah (Hebrew); diminutive forms are *Jodie, Judy*.

**Julia** fem form of Julius; a variant form is *Juliana*; a diminutive form is *Julie*.

**Julie, Juliet** diminutive forms of Julia, now used independently.

**Julienne** fem form of Julien.

**Julieta** a Spanish form of Julia.

**Juliette** the French form of Julia, now used as an English-language form.

**Jumaana** silver pearl (Indian).

**June** the name of the month used as a first name (Latin).

**Juno** queen of heaven, in Roman mythology the equivalent of Hera (Latin).

**Justina** the Spanish form of Justine.

**Justine** fem form of Justin, Justus.

**Jyoti** light (Indian).

# K

**Kaamla** perfect (Indian).

**Kajri** light as a cloud (Indian).

**Kalantha, Kalanthe** variant forms of Calantha.

**Kali Kajal** eyeliner (Hindu).

**Kalyani** fortunate (Indian).

**Kalypso** a variant form of Calypso.

**Kameela** most perfect (Indian).

**Kamna** desire (Hindu).

**Kanchana** a celestial Apsara, gold (Hindu).

**Kara** a variant form of Cara.

**Karen** a Dutch and Scandinavian form of Katherine.

**Karin** a Scandinavian form of Katherine.

**Karla** fem form of Karl.

**Karlotte** a German form of Charlotte.

**Karoline** a German form of Caroline.

**Karunya** compassionate (Indian).

**Katerina** a variant form of Katherine.

**Katharina, Katharine** German forms of Katherine; a diminutive form is *Katrine*.

**Katherine** pure (Greek); diminutive forms are *Kate, Kath, Katie, Katy, Kay, Kit, Kittie*.

**Kathleen** an Irish form of Katherine.

**Kathryn** an American form of Katherine.

**Katinka** a Russian form of Katherine.

**Katrine** a diminutive form of Katharina; a variant form of Katriona.

**Katriona** a variant form of Catriona; a variant form is *Katrine*.

**Kausalya** Mother of Rama (Hindu).

**Kavita** poem (Hindu).

**Kayla, Kayleigh, Kayley** derivation uncertain, possibly slender (Irish Gaelic), a combination of Kay and Leigh, or a variant form of Kelly.

**Keely** beautiful (Gaelic).

**Keira** a variant spelling of Ciara.

**Kelly** a surname, meaning descendant of war, used as a first name (Irish Gaelic).

**Kendra** fem form of Kendrick.

**Kerry** the name of the Irish county, used as a first name.

**Keturah** incense (Hebrew).

**Kezia, Keziah** the cassia tree (Hebrew); diminutive forms are *Kizzie, Kizzy*.

**Kimberley** a surname, meaning wood clearing, used as a first name (Old English); a diminutive form is *Kim*.

**Kinjal** river bank (Indian).

**Kirstel** a German form of Christine.

**Kirsten** a Scandinavian form of Christine.

**Kirstie, Kirsty** a diminutive form of Kirstin, used independently.

**Kirstin** a Scots form of Christine; a diminutive form is *Kirstie*.

**Kirti** fame, a form of the Devi (Hindu).

**Kittie, Kitty** diminutive forms of Katherine.

**Kizzie, Kizzy** diminutive forms of Kezia.

**Klara** the German form of Clara.

**Komali** tender (Indian).

**Kora** a variant form of Cora.

**Krisha** divine (Indian).

**Kristeen** a variant form of Christine.

**Kristina** the Swedish form of Christina.

**Kriti** a work of art (Hindu).

**Kshama** forgiveness, patience (Hindu)

**Kulthoom** daughter of the prophet Mohammed (Indian).

**Kuvira** courageous woman (Indian).

**Kylie** a combination of Kyle and Kelly.

**Kyrena** a variant form of Cyrena.

# L

**Laboni** graceful (Indian).

**Lacey** a surname, meaning from Lassy in the Calvados region of Normandy, used as a first name (Old French).

**Ladli** loved one (Indian).

**Laetitia** happiness (Latin); variant forms are *Latisha*, *Letitia*.

**Lajita** modest (Indian).

**Lakshanya** one who achieves (Indian).

**Lakshmi** goddess, consort of Lord Vishnu (Hindu).

**Lalita** goddess, form of Parvati, consort of Lord Shiva (Hindu).

**Lana** a variant form of Alana.

**Lara** a diminutive form of Larissa (Latin).

**Laraine** a variant form of Lorraine; the queen (Old French).

**Laranya** graceful (Indian).

**Larissa, Larisa** meaning uncertain, possibly happy as a lark (Greek/Russian); diminutive forms are *Lara, Lissa*.

**Lateefa** gentle (Indian).

**Laura** laurel, bay tree (Latin); a diminutive form is *Laurie*.

**Laurel** a name for the evergreen bay tree, used as a first name.

**Lauren** fem form of Laurence; a variant form is *Loren*; a diminutive form is *Laurie*.

**Laurette** a French form of Laura; a variant form is *Lauretta*.

**Lavender** the English name of the plant that bears blue or mauve flowers, used as a first name.

**Laverne** the alder tree (Old French); diminutive forms are *Verna, Verne*.

**Lavinia, Lavina** of Latium in Italy (Latin).

**Laxmi** goddess of wealth (Indian).

**Lea** a variant form of Leah, Lee.

**Leah** languid, or wild cow (Hebrew); variant forms are *Lea, Lee*.

**Leanne** a combination of Lee and Anne; a variant form is *Leane*.

**Leanora, Leanore** German variant forms of Eleanor.

**Leda** mother of beauty.

**Leena** tender (Indian).

**Lela** a variant form of Leila.

**Lena** a diminutive form of Helena.

**Lenora** a variant form of Leonora.

**Leonie** fem form of Leo, Leon; a variant form is *Leona*.

**Leonora** an Italian form of Eleanor; a variant form is *Lenora*; a diminutive form is *Nora*.

**Leslie** a surname, meaning garden by water, used as a first name (Gaelic).

**Leticia, Letitia** variant forms of Laetitia.

**Liana, Liane, Lianna, Lianne** sun (Greek); variant forms are *Leane, Leana, Leanna*.

**Lila** a variant form of Leila; a diminutive form of Delilah.

**Lilac** bluish (Persian), the English name of the syringa plant with fragrant purple or white flowers, used as a first name.

**Lilah** a variant form of Leila; a diminutive form of Delilah.

**Lilian** a diminutive form of Elizabeth; a variant form of Lily; a variant form is *Lillian*.

**Lilias, Lillias** Scottish forms of Lilian.

**Lilibet** a diminutive form of Elizabeth.

**Lilie** a German form of Lily; a variant form is *Lili*.

**Lilith** of the night (Hebrew).

**Lily** the name of the flowering plant with showy blossoms, used as a first name; a variant form is *Lilli*; a diminutive form is *Lil*.

**Linda** a diminutive form of Belinda, Rosalind, etc., now used independently; a variant form is *Lynda*; diminutive forms are *Lin, Lindie, Lindy*.

**Lindsay, Lindsey** a surname, meaning island of Lincoln, used as a first name; variant forms are *Linsay, Linsey, Linzi, Lynsay, Lynsey*.

**Lisa** a diminutive form of Elizabeth, now used independently; a variant form is *Liza*.

**Lisette** a diminutive form of Louise.

**Lissa** a diminutive form of Larissa, Melissa.

**Livia** a variant form of Olivia.

**Lochan** bright eyes (Indian).

**Lois** meaning uncertain, possibly good, desirable (Greek).

**Lola** a diminutive form of

Dolores, Carlotta, now used independently.

**Lolaksi** a sakti of Ganesha (Hindu).

**Lona** a diminutive form of Maelona.

**Lora** a Welsh form of Laura.

**Lorelei** the name of a rock in the River Rhine from where, in German legend, a siren lured boatmen.

**Loren** a variant form of Lauren.

**Lorna** a name invented by R. D. Blackmore, possibly from Lorne, for the heroine of his novel Lorna Doone.

**Lorraine** a surname meaning man from Lorraine (bold and famous) used as a first name (Old French); a variant form is *Laraine*.

**Lottie, Lotty** diminutive forms of Charlotte.

**Lotus** the English name of a fruit that in Greek mythology was said to induce langour and forgetfulness.

**Louella** a combination of Louise and Ella.

**Louisa** fem form of Louis.

**Louise** the French form of Louisa, now used widely as an English-language form; diminutive forms are *Lisette, Lou*.

**Lucia** fem form of Lucian.

**Lucienne** fem form of Lucien.

**Lucilla** a diminutive form of Lucia.

**Lucinda** a variant form of Lucia; a diminutive form is *Cindy*.

**Lucretia, Lucrece** from lucrum, gain (Latin).

**Lucy** a popular form of Lucia; a diminutive form is *Luce*.

**Ludmila, Ludmilla** of the people (Russian).

**Luella** a variant form of Louella.

**Luisa** an Italian and Spanish form of Louisa.

**Luise** the German form of Louisa; a diminutive form is *Lulu*.

**Lynda** a variant form of Linda; diminutive forms are *Lyn, Lynn, Lynne*.

**Lynette** an English form of Eluned; variant forms are *Lynnette, Linnette*.

**Lynn** pool or waterfall (Celtic); also a diminutive form of Lynda; a variant form is *Lynne*.

**Lyris** she who plays the harp (Greek).

**Lysandra** fem form of Lysander.

# M

**Mabel** a diminutive form of Amabel, also used independently; a variant form is *Maybelle*.

**Mabelle** a French form of Mabel.

**Madalena** the Spanish form of Madeleine.

**Maddalena** the Italian form of Madeleine.

**Maddie, Maddy** diminutive forms of Madeleine.

**Madeleine, Madeline** from Magdala on the Sea of Galilee (French); a variant form is *Magdalene*; diminutive forms are *Maddie, Maddy, Mala*.

**Madge** diminutive forms of Margaret, Marjory.

**Madhuvanthi** one who is sweet like honey (Indian).

**Madonna** my lady, a title of the Virgin Mary (Italian).

**Mae** a variant form of May.

**Maelona** princess (Welsh).

**Maeve** intoxicating (Celtic); variant forms are *Mave, Meave*.

**Magda** a German and Scandinavian form of Magdalene.

**Magnolia** the name of a tree with showy flowers, named after the French botanist Pierre Magnol, used as a first name.

**Mahalia** tenderness (Hebrew).

**Mai, Mair** Welsh forms of May.

**Maida** the name of a place in Calabria in Spain, where a battle was fought in 1806, used as a first name; a diminutive form is *Maidie*.

**Mairead** an Irish form of Margaret.

**Mairi** Scots Gaelic form of Mary.

**Maisie** diminutive forms of Margaret, also used independently.

**Mala** a diminutive form of Madeleine.

**Malvina** smooth brow (Scots Gaelic).

**Mamta** mother's love for child (Hindu).

**Manette** a French form of Mary.

**Manika** jewel (Indian).

**Manjusha** lady with a sweet voice (Indian).

**Manuela** God with us (Spanish).

**Marcela** a Spanish form of Marcella.

**Marcella** fem form of Marcellus.

**Marcelle** a French form of Marcella.

**Marcia** form of Marcius; a variant form is *Marsha*; diminutive forms are *Marcie, Marcy.*

**Mared** a Welsh form of Margaret.

**Margaret** a pearl (Greek); diminutive forms are *Greta, Madge, Maggie, Margie, May, Meg, Meggie, Meta, Peg.*

**Margarete** the Danish and German form of Margaret; diminutive forms are *Grete, Gretchen.*

**Margaretha** a Dutch form of Margaret.

**Margarita** the Spanish form of Margaret; a diminutive form is *Rita.*

**Margaux** a variant form of Margot.

**Margery** in the Middle Ages a diminutive form of Margaret, but now a name in its own right; a variant form is *Marjorie*; a diminutive form is *Madge, Marge.*

**Margherita** the Italian form of

Margaret; a diminutive form is *Rita.*

**Margo, Margot** diminutive forms of Margaret, Marguerite, now used independently; a variant form is *Margaux.*

**Marguerite** the French form of Margaret; diminutive forms are *Margo, Margot.*

**Mari** an Irish and Welsh form of Mary.

**Maria** the Latin, Italian, German and Spanish form of Mary; a diminutive form is *Ria.*

**Mariam** the Greek form of Mary.

**Marian** a French form of Marion.

**Marianna** an Italian form of Marianne, Marion.

**Marianne** a French and German form of Marion; a compound of Mary and Ann.

**Maribella** a compound of Mary and Bella.

**Marie** a French form of Mary; a diminutive form is *Marion.*

**Marietta** diminutive form of Maria, also used independently.

**Marigold** the name of the golden flower, used as a first name.

**Marilyn** diminutive form of

Mary, also used independently.

**Marina** of the sea (Latin).

**Marion** a variant form of Mary.

**Marisa** summit (Hebrew), mother of Daksa (Hindu).

**Marlene** a contraction of Maria Magdalena (German).

**Marsha** a variant form of Marcia.

**Marta** the Italian, Spanish and Swedish form of Martha, now used as an English-language form; a variant form is *Martita*.

**Martha** lady (Hebrew); diminutive forms are *Mat, Mattie*.

**Marthe** the French and German form of Martha.

**Marti** a diminutive form of Martina, Martine.

**Martina** fem form of Martin; a diminutive form is *Marti*.

**Martine** the French form of Martina, now used as an English-language form; a diminutive form is *Marti*.

**Martita** a variant form of Marta; a diminutive form is *Tita*.

**Mary** bitter; their rebellion; star of the sea (Hebrew); variant forms are *Marion, Miriam*; diminutive forms are *Mamie, May, Minnie, Mollie, Polly*.

**Maryann, Maryanne** compounds

of Mary and Ann or Anne.

**Marylou** a compound of Mary and Louise.

**Matangi** a Devi (Hindu).

**Mathilda** a variant form of Matilda.

**Mathilde** the French form of Matilda.

**Matilda** mighty war (Germanic); a variant form is *Mathilda*; diminutive forms are *Mat, Mattie, Tilda, Tilly*.

**Matilde** the Italian and Spanish form of Matilda.

**Maud, Maude** a medieval form of Matilda.

**Maura** an Irish form of Mary.

**Maureen** an Irish diminutive form of Mary.

**Mave** a variant form of Maeve; a diminutive form of Mavis.

**Mavis** an alternative name of the song thrush, used as a first name (English); a diminutive form is *Mave*.

**Maxine** fem form of Max.

**May** diminutive form of Margaret, Mary; the name of the month, used as a first name; a variant form is *Mae*; a diminutive form is *Minnie*.

**Maya** illusion (Indian).

**Maybelle** a compound of May

and Belle; a variant form of Mabel.

**Maysoon** of beautiful face and body (Indian).

**Meave** a variant form of Maeve.

**Medea** meditative; in Greek mythology the princess who helped Jason obtain the Golden Fleece from her father (Greek).

**Medha** intelligence (Hindu).

**Meena** precious stone (Hindu).

**Megan** Welsh diminutive form of Meg, now used independently.

**Melanie** black (Greek).

**Melinda** honey (Greek) plus the suffix -inda.

**Melisande** the French form of Millicent.

**Melissa** a bee (Greek); a diminutive form is *Lissa*.

**Melody** a word for tune or tunefulness, used as a first name.

**Mena** mother of Menaka (Hindu).

**Menaka** celestial damsel (Hindu).

**Mercedes** the Spanish form of Mercy (as a plural).

**Mercy** the quality of forgiveness, used as a first name (English).

**Meredith** a surname, meaning

lord, used as a first name (Welsh).

**Meri** a variant form of Merry.

**Meriel** a Welsh form of Muriel; variant forms are *Merle, Meryl*.

**Meryl** a variant form of Meriel, Merrill.

**Meta** a diminutive form of Margaret.

**Mia** a diminutive form of Maria.

**Michaela** fem form of Michael.

**Michaella** the Italian form of Michaela.

**Michèle, Michelle** French forms of Michaela, now used as English-language forms.

**Mignon** a word, meaning sweet, dainty, used as a first name (French); diminutive forms are *Mignonette, Minette*.

**Mil** a diminutive form of Mildred, Millicent.

**Milcah** queen (Hebrew).

**Mildred** gentle counsel (Germanic); diminutive forms are *Mil, Millie*.

**Millicent** work and strength (Germanic); a diminutive form is *Millie*.

**Millie** diminutive form of Amelia, Emilia, Mildred, Millicent.

**Mimi** an Italian diminutive form of Maria.

**Mimosa** the English name of a tropical shrub with yellow flowers, used as a first name, from imitative (Latin).

**Minerva** wise one; in Roman mythology the counterpart of Athena, goddess of wisdom.

**Minna, Minne** love (Germanic); diminutive forms of Wilhelmina.

**Minnie** a diminutive form of Mary, May, Wilhelmina.

**Minta** a diminutive form of Araminta.

**Mirabel, Mirabelle** wonderful (Latin); diminutive forms are *Mira, Myra*.

**Miranda** wonderful (Latin); diminutive forms are *Mira, Myra*.

**Miriam** variant form of Mary.

**Mishti** sweet person (Indian).

**Mitzi** a German diminutive form of Maria.

**Modesty** an English word from modestus (Latin) for the quality of being shy or humble, used as a first name.

**Mohini** most beautiful (Hindu).

**Moira** an anglicized Irish form of Mary; a variant form is *Moyra*.

**Mollie, Molly** diminutive forms of Mary, now used independently.

**Mona** noble (Irish Gaelic).

**Monica** of uncertain meaning, but possibly advising (Latin).

**Monika** the German form of Monica.

**Monique** the French form of Monica, now also used as an English form.

**Morag** great (Scots Gaelic).

**Morna** a Scots variant form of Myrna.

**Morven** a Scottish placename, meaning sea gap, used as a first name (Scots Gaelic).

**Muriel** sea bright (Celtic).

**Musheera** giving counsel (Indian).

**Myfanwy** my fine one (Welsh).

**Myra** a name invented by the poet Fulke Greville, possibly as an anagram of Mary, or to mean she who laments (Greek); a diminutive form of Mirabel, Miranda.

**Myrna** beloved (Irish Gaelic); a variant form is Morna.

**Myrtle** the name of the shrub, used as a first name.

# N

**Naamah** pretty, loved (Hebrew).

**Nabeeha** intelligent (Indian).

**Nadezhda** hope (Russian).

**Nadia** an English, French and Italian form of Nadezhda.

**Nadine** a French variant form of Nadia.

**Nadira** rare; precious (Indian).

**Naida** the water nymph (Latin); a variant form is Naiada.

**Naija** daughter of wisdom (Indian).

**Nairne** from the river (Gaelic).

**Nana** a diminutive form of Hannah.

**Nancy** a variant form of Ann, now used independently; diminutive forms are *Nan, Nina*.

**Nanette** a variant form of Ann, now used independently; a diminutive form is *Nan*.

**Naomi** pleasantness (Hebrew).

**Nara** nearest and dearest (English).

**Narda** fragrant perfume. The lingering essence (Latin).

**Nashita** energetic and full of life (Indian).

**Natalia** a Spanish form of Natalya.

**Natalie** a French form of Natalya now used as an English-language form.

**Natalya** Christmas (Latin/Russian).

**Natasha** a Russian diminutive form of Natalya.

**Nathania** gift of God (Hebrew); diminutive forms are *Natene, Nathene, Nathane*.

**Nazaaha** purity, righteousness, honesty (Indian).

**Neale** fem form of Neil.

**Nell, Nellie, Nelly** diminutive forms of Eleanor, Ellen, Helen.

**Nerice, Nerima, Nerine, Nerissa** from the sea (Greek).

**Nerys** lord (Welsh).

**Nessa** a diminutive form of Agnes, Vanessa.

**Nessie** a diminutive form of Agnes.

**Nesta** a Welsh diminutive form of Agnes.

**Netta, Nettie** diminutive forms of Henrietta.

**Niamh** bright (Irish Gaelic).

**Nicole** fem form of Nicholas; variant forms are *Nicola, Nicolette, Colette*; diminutive forms are *Nicky, Nikkie*.

**Nidra** a form of the Devi (Hindu).

**Nikita** earth (Indian).

**Nikki** a diminutive form of Nicole.

**Nina** a diminutive form of Nancy; beautiful eyes (Indian).

**Ninette** (French) a variant form of Ann.

**Ninon** a variant form of Ann (French).

**Nisha** night (Hindu).

**Nita** a diminutive form of Anita, Juanita.

**Nitya** goddess Parvati (Hindu).

**Nixie** water sprite (Germanic); diminutive forms are *Nissie, Nissy*.

**Noël, Noel** Christmas (French).

**Noëlle, Noelle** form of Noël.

**Nola** famous (Irish Gaelic).

**Nona** ninth (Latin).

**Noor** light (Indian).

**Nora, Norah** a diminutive form of Eleanor, Honora, Leonora, also used independently.

**Noreen** an Irish form of Nora.

**Norma** a rule (Latin), but probably invented as the name of the heroine of Bellini's opera.

**Nuala** a diminutive form of Fionnuala, also used independently.

**Octavia** fem form of Octavius.

**Octavie** a French form of Octavia.

**Odelia, Odelie** variant forms of Odile.

**Odette** fem form of Oda.

**Odile, Odille** rich, wealthy (Germanic); variant forms are *Odelia, Odelie, Ottilie, Otilie*.

**Oditi** dawn (Indian).

**Ofra** a variant form of Ophrah.

**Olga** the Russian form of Helga.

**Olimpia** the Italian form of Olympia.

**Olive** an olive (Latin); a variant form is *Olivia*.

**Olivia** a variant form of Olive; a diminutive form is *Livia*.

**Olwen** white track (Welsh).

**Olympe** the French form of Olympia.

**Olympia** heavenly (Greek).

**Omaja** result of spiritual unity (Indian).

**Omisha** goddess of birth and death (Indian).

**Ona** a diminutive form of names ending -ona, e.g. Fiona.

**Oni** shelter (Indian).

**Oona, Oonagh** variant forms of Una.

**Opal** the name of the iridescent gemstone, used as a first name, precious stone (Sanskrit).

**Ophelia** from ophis, serpent (Greek).

**Ophélie** the French form of Ophelia.

**Ophrah, Ophra** fawn (Hebrew); variant forms are *Ofra, Oprah*.

**Oprah** a modern variant of Ophrah.

**Oriana, Oriane** golden (Latin).

**Oriel** strife (Germanic).

**Orla** golden girl (Irish Gaelic).

**Orlanda** fem form of Orlando.

**Orna** fem form of Oran.

**Orsola** the Italian form of Ursula.

**Ortensia** the Italian form of Hortense.

**Ottavia** the Italian form of Octavia.

**Ottilie, Otilie** variant forms of Odile.

# P

**Paige, Page** a surname, meaning page, used as a first name (Old French).

**Paloma** the Spanish word for dove, used as a first name.

**Pamela** a name invented by the poet Sir Philip Sidney for his work Arcadia, derived from the Greek work for honey; a diminutive form is *Pam*.

**Panchali** princess (Indian).

**Pandora** gifted (Greek); in Greek mythology, the first woman on earth.

**Panna** emerald (Indian).

**Pansy** thought (French); the name of the garden flower, used as a first name.

**Paola** the Italian form of Paula.

**Parmita** wisdom (Indian).

**Parvati** wife of Lord Shiva (Indian).

**Patience** patience (Latin).

**Patricia** fem form of Patrick; diminutive forms are *Paddy, Pat, Patsy, Pattie, Patty, Tricia*.

**Patrizia** the Italian form of Patricia.

**Pattie, Patty** diminutive forms of Martha, Patience, Patricia.

**Paula** fem form of Paul.

**Paulette** a French form of Paula.

**Peace** the word for the condition of tranquillity or calm, used as a first name (Latin).

**Pearl** the name of the lustrous white gem, used as a first name.

**Peg, Peggie, Peggy** diminutive forms of Margaret.

**Penelope** duck (Greek); diminutive forms are *Pen, Penny*.

**Peony** healing (Greek), the name of a plant with pink, red, white or yellow flowers, used as a first name.

**Perdita** lost (Latin), invented by Shakespeare for a character in The Winter's Tale.

**Peronel** contraction of Petronel.

**Persephone** of uncertain meaning; in Greek mythology, goddess of the underworld (Greek).

**Persis** a Persian woman (Greek).

**Petra** fem form of Peter.

**Petrina** a diminutive form of Petra.

**Petronel, Petronella** form of Petronius, a Roman family name (Latin).

**Petula** asking (Latin); a diminutive form is *Pet*.

**Petunia** the name of a plant with white, blue or purple flowers, used as a first name.

**Phebe** a variant form of Phoebe.

**Phedra** bright (Greek).

**Phèdre** the French form of Phedra.

**Phemie, Phamie** diminutive forms of Euphemia.

**Phenie** a diminutive form of Josephine.

**Philippa** fem form of Philip; diminutive forms are *Phil, Pippa*.

**Philomena** love and strength (Greek).

**Phoebe** moon (Greek); a variant form is *Phebe*.

**Phyllida** a variant form of Phyllis.

**Phyllis** a green bough (Greek).

**Pia** pious (Latin).

**Pilar** pillar (Spanish), an allusion to the Virgin Mary who appeared to St James the Greater, standing on a pillar.

**Pippa** a diminutive form of Philippa.

**Pivari** a wife of Sukha (Hindu).

**Polly** diminutive form of Mary, now used independently.

**Pollyanna** a compound of Polly and Anna.

**Pomona** fruitful (Latin).

**Pooja** prayer (Hindu).

**Poonam** full moon (Indian).

**Poppy** the name of the plant that has a bright red flower, used as a first name.

**Portia** gift (Latin).

**Prajakta** fragrant flower (Indian).

**Prarthana** prayer (Indian).

**Prima** fem form of Primo.

**Primrose** the name of the yellow spring flower, used as a first name.

**Priscilla** from prisca, ancient (Latin); diminutive forms are *Cilla, Prissie*.

**Prudence** the word for the quality of caution or circumspection, used as a first name (Latin); diminutive forms are *Prue, Prudie*.

**Prunella** plum (Latin); a diminutive form is *Prue*.

**Punita** holy (Indian).

**Pusti** nourishment (Hindu).

**Queenie** a diminutive form of the word queen, the supreme woman, used as a first name (Old English).

**Quenby** a surname, meaning queen's manor, used as a first name (Old English).

**Querida** beloved, a Spanish term of endearment, used as a first name.

**Quinta** fem form of Quinto; a variant form is *Quintina* (Latin).

# R

**Rabhya** worshipped (Indian).

**Rachel** lamb (Hebrew); a variant form is *Rachelle*; diminutive forms are *Rae, Ray*.

**Rachele** the Italian form of Rachel.

**Rachelle** a variant form of Rachel.

**Radhika** a form of the Devi, 5th Sakti, wife of Krishna (Hindu).

**Rae** a diminutive form of Rachel.

**Raquel** the Spanish form of Rachel.

**Rasheeda** wise (Indian).

**Rati** a Devi (Hindu).

**Raveena** sunny (Indian).

**Raven** the name of a bird, used as a first name.

**Rayne** a surname, meaning mighty army, used as a first name; a variant form is Raine.

**Rea** a variant form of Rhea.

**Rebecca, Rebekah** the Hebrew word means noose and the name has come to mean bound, faithful; diminutive forms are *Beckie, Becky*.

**Regina** queen (Latin).

**Reine** queen (French).

**Rekha** straight line (Hindu).

**Renata** a diminutive form of Renée.

**Renée** fem form of René.

**Rexanne** a compound of Rex and Anne; a variant form of Roxanne.

**Rhea, Rheia** of uncertain origin and meaning; in Roman mythology she was the mother of Remus and Romulus; in Greek mythology she was the mother of several gods, including Zeus; a variant form is Rea.

**Rhiannon** goddess (Welsh).

**Rhoda** rose (Greek).

**Rhona** a variant form of Rona.

**Ria** a German diminutive form of Maria.

**Rina** a diminutive form of names ending -rina.

**Rishima** moonbeam (Indian).

**Rita** a diminutive form of Margarita, Margherita, used independently.

**Roberta** fem form of Robert.

**Robina** fem form of Robin.

**Rochelle** little rock (French).

**Roderica** fem form of Roderick; a variant form is Rodericka; a diminutive form is Rica.

**Rohann**a fem form of Rohan.

**Róisín, Roisin** an Irish form of Rose.

**Rolanda, Rolande** fem forms of Roland.

**Roma** a Roman (Latin).

**Romy** a diminutive form of Rosemary.

**Rona** the name of a Scottish island, meaning rough rocky island, used as a first name (Old Norse); a variant form is *Rhona*.

**Rosa** a rose (Latin); diminutive forms are *Rosetta, Rosie*.

**Rosabel, Rosabella, Rosabelle** a compound of Rosa and Bella.

**Rosalie, Rosalia** little and blooming rose.

**Rosalind, Rosaline** beautiful as a rose (Latin); a diminutive form is *Linda*.

**Rosamund, Rosamond** rose of the world (Latin).

**Rosanne, Rosanna** compounds of Rose and Anne; variant forms are *Roseanne, Roseanna*.

**Rose** the English form of Rosa; the name of the flower, used as a first name; diminutive forms are *Rosette, Rosie*.

**Rosemarie** a combination of Rose and Marie.

**Rosemary** the name of the plant associated with remembrance, used as a first name; diminutive forms are *Romy, Rosie*.

**Rosemonde** a French form of Rosamund.

**Rosetta** a diminutive form of Rosa.

**Rosette** a diminutive form of Rose.

**Roshni** light (Hindu).

**Rosie** a diminutive form of Rosa, Rose, Rosemary, now also used independently.

**Rosmunda** the Italian form of Rosamund.

**Rowena** fame and joy (Germanic).

**Roxanne, Roxane** dawn of day (Persian); a variant form is *Rexanne*; a diminutive form is *Roxie*.

**Ruby** the name of the red gemstone, used as a first name.

**Ruth** friend (Hebrew).

# S

**Sabina** Sabine woman (Latin).

**Sabine** a French and German form of Sabina.

**Sabra** restful (Hebrew).

**Sabrina** of uncertain meaning, linked to the name of the River Severn (pre-Celtic); a variant form is Zabrina.

**Sachi** wife of Indra (Hindu); grace (Indian).

**Sadie** a diminutive form of Sara.

**Salina** from the salty place (Greek).

**Sally, Sallie** diminutive forms of Sara, now used independently.

**Salome** peaceful (Hebrew).

**Salvia** sage (Latin).

**Samantha** meaning obscure, possibly listener (Aramaic) or a compound of Sam and Anthea; a diminutive form is Sam.

**Samuela** fem form of Samuel.

**Sandra** a diminutive form of Alessandra, Alexandra, now used independently.

**Sanjna** wife of the Sun (Hindu).

**Sapna** dream (Hindu).

**Sapphire** from saphir, beautiful (Hebrew); the name of the blue precious stone, used as a first name.

**Sarah, Sara** princess (Hebrew); diminutive forms are Sadie, Sal, Sally.

**Savanna** a form of the word for an open grassland, used as a first name (Spanish).

**Savarna** daughter of the Ocean (Hindu).

**Savita** sun (Hindu).

**Scarlett** a variation of the word scarlet, a bright red colour.

**Selina, Selena** parsley; heavenly (Greek); a diminutive form is Lina.

**Selma** fem form of Anselm.

**Senga** slender (Gaelic).

**Seonaid** a Gaelic form of Janet.

**Septima** fem form of Septimus.

**Seraphina, Serafina** of the seraphim, of burning faith (Hebrew).

**Shannon** the name of the Irish river, meaning the old one, used as a first name.

**Shari** a diminutive form of Sharon.

**Sharon** a Biblical placename mentioned in the Song of Solomon, used as a first name

(Hebrew); a diminutive form is *Shari*.

**Sheelagh** a variant form of Sheila.

**Sheelah** petition (Hebrew); a variant form of Sheila.

**Sheena** an anglicized form of Sine.

**Sheila, Shelagh** anglicized forms of Sile; variant forms are *Sheelagh, Sheelah*.

**Shelley** a surname, meaning clearing on a bank, used as a first name (Old English).

**Sheree, Sheri** variant forms of Chérie.

**Sheryl** a variant form of Cheryl.

**Shirley** a surname and placename, meaning thin clearing, used as a first name; a diminutive form is Shirl.

**Shona** the anglicized form of Seonaid.

**Sian** the Welsh form of Jane.

**Sibeal** an Irish form of Sybyl.

**Sibyl, Sibylla** soothsayer (Greek); variant forms are *Sybyl, Sybylla*; a diminutive form is *Sib*.

**Sidney** a surname, meaning wide island, used as a first name; a variant form is *Sydney*; a diminutive form is Sid.

**Sierra** the name for a mountain range, used as a first name (Spanish).

**Sigrid** fair and victorious (Old Norse); a diminutive form is *Siri*.

**Sile** the Gaelic form of Celia, Cecily, often rendered in English as Sheila, Shelagh, etc.

**Silvana** fem form of Silvano.

**Silvia** of a wood (Latin); a variant form is *Sylvia*.

**Silvie** the French form of Silvia.

**Simona** fem form of Simon; a diminutive form is Sim.

**Simone** the French form of Simona.

**Sine** a Gaelic form of Jane, often rendered in English as Sheena.

**Sinead** an Irish Gaelic form of Janet.

**Siobhan** an Irish Gaelic form of Jane.

**Sioned** a Welsh form of Janet.

**Sisley** a variant form of Cecily; diminutive forms are *Sis, Sissie, Sissy*.

**Sofie** the French form of Sophie.

**Sonya, Sonia** a Russian diminutive form of Sophia.

**Sophia** wisdom (Greek).

**Sorcha** bright one (Irish Gaelic).

**Spring** desire (Sanskrit).

**Stacy, Stacie** diminutive forms of Eustacia, Anastasia, now used independently.

**Star, Starr** an English form of Stella.

**Stasia** a diminutive form of Anastasia.

**Steffi, Steffie** diminutive forms of Stephanie.

**Stella** star (Latin).

**Stephanie** fem form of Stephen; a diminutive form is *Stevie*.

**Storm** the word for a meteorological condition, used as a first name (Old English).

**Suha** name of a star (Indian).

**Sukey, Sukie** diminutive forms of Susan.

**Summer** season (Sanskrit).

**Susan** the English form of Susanna; diminutive forms are *Sue, Sukey, Sukie, Susie, Susy*.

**Susanna, Susannah** lily (Hebrew); a variant form is *Suzanna*.

**Susanne** a German form of Susanna.

**Suvali** (Indian) full of grace.

**Suzanne** a French and German form of Susan.

**Sybille** the French form of Sybil.

**Sybyl, Sybilla** variant forms of Sibyl, Sibylla; a diminutive form is *Syb*.

**Sylvia** a variant form of Silvia.

**Sylvie** the French form of Silvia.

# T

**Tabitha** gazelle (Aramaic); diminutive forms are *Tab, Tabby*.

**Talitha** maiden (Aramaic).

**Tallulah** a placename, meaning spring water, used as a first name (North American Indian).

**Tamanna** wish (Indian).

**Tamar** palm tree (Hebrew); diminutive forms are *Tammie, Tammy*.

**Tamara** the Russian form of Tamar.

**Tammie, Tammy** diminutive forms of Tamar, Tamsin.

**Tamsin** a Cornish contraction of Thomasina, now used independently; a diminutive form is *Tammie*.

**Tania, Tanya** diminutive forms of Tatiana, Titania.

**Tanisha** born on Monday (Hausa); ambition (Indian).

**Tansy** immortal (Greek), the name of a medicinal plant bearing yellow flowers, used as a first name.

**Tara** a placename, meaning rocky assembly place, used as a first name; in Irish history, the site of ancient royal power (Irish Gaelic).

**Tatiana** form of a Roman family, name of unknown meaning (Latin); diminutive forms are *Tania, Tanya*.

**Tavishi** courage (Indian).

**Tejasvi** brilliant (Indian).

**Tempest** the word for a violent storm, used as a first name (Latin).

**Teodora** an Italian and Spanish form of Theodora.

**Teodosia** an Italian form of Theodosia.

**Teresa** the Italian and Spanish forms of Theresa.

**Terese** a variant form of Theresa.

**Teri** a diminutive form of Theresa.

**Terri** a diminutive form of Teresa, Theresa, now used independently.

**Terry** a diminutive form of Teresa.

**Tess, Tessa, Tessie** diminutive forms of Esther, Teresa, Theresa.

**Thalia** flourishing blossom (Greek).

**Thea** a diminutive form of Althea, Dorothea, now used independently.

**Thecla** god glory (Greek).

**Theda** a diminutive form of Theodora, Theodosia.

**Thelma** a name coined in the 19th century by Marie Corelli for her novel Thelma; possibly derived from wish (Greek).

**Theodora** fem form of Theodore; diminutive forms are *Dora, Theo*.

**Theodosia** gift of God (Greek).

**Theresa** carrying ears of corn (Greek); diminutive forms are *Teri, Terri, Terry, Tess, Tessa, Tessie, Tracey, Tracie, Tracy*.

**Thérèse** the French form of Theresa.

**Theresia, Therese** German forms of Theresa.

**Thomasina, Thomasine** fem forms of Thomas.

**Thyrza** a variant form of Thirza.

**Tib, Tibbie** (Scots) diminutive forms of Isabel, Isabella.

**Tiffany** the manifestation of God, the festival of Epiphany (Greek).

**Tilda, Tilde** diminutive forms of Matilda.

**Tilly** a diminutive form of Matilda.

**Timothea** fem form of Timothy.

**Tina** a diminutive form of Christina, Christine, etc., also used independently.

**Tiree** the name of an island, meaning land of corn, used as a first name (Scots Gaelic).

**Tirza, Tirzah** variant forms of Thirza.

**Tisya** auspicious (Indian).

**Tita** fem form of Titus; a diminutive form of Martita.

**Titania** giant, in medieval folklore wife of Oberon and queen of fairies (Greek); diminutive forms are *Tania, Tanya.*

**Tomasina, Tomina** fem forms of Thomas.

**Toni** diminutive forms of *Annette, Antoinette, Antonia*, now used independently.

**Tonia** a diminutive form of Antonia.

**Tonie** diminutive forms of Annette, Antoinette, Antonia, now used independently.

**Topaz** the name of a white gemstone, sometimes used as a first name.

**Trisha** a diminutive form of Patricia.

**Trista** sorrowful (Latin).

**Trix, Trixie** diminutive forms of Beatrice.

**Truda, Trudie, Trudy** diminutive forms of Gertrude.

**Tuesday** day of Mars (Old English.

# U

**Uda** fem form of Udo.

**Ulrica** English form of Ulrike.

**Ulrike** fem form of Ulrich.

**Una** a lamb; hunger (Irish Gaelic); form of one (Latin), used by Edmund Spenser in The Faerie Queene.

**Unity** the quality of harmony or concord, used as a first name.

**Urania** heavenly – the name of

one of the Muses (Greek).

**Ursula** she-bear (Latin).

**Ursule** the French form of Ursula.

**Urvasi** most beautiful of Apsaras (Hindu).

**Uttara** mother of Pariksit (Hindu).

**Valborga** protecting ruler (Germanic); diminutive forms are *Walburga, Walborga, Valburga*.

**Valentina** fem form of Valentine; a diminutive form is *Val*.

**Valentine** strong; healthy; powerful (Latin); a diminutive form is Val.

**Valerie** strong (Latin); a diminutive form is *Val*.

**Vanessa** from the New Latin word to mean butterfly; a diminutive form is *Nessa*.

**Varsha** rain (Hindu).

**Varuni** a goddess (Hindu).

**Vasanta** spring (Hindu).

**Vasavi** mental daughter of the Pitrs (Hindu).

**Venetia** the name of the region around Venice in northern Italy, used as a first name (Latin).

**Vera** faith (Russian); true (Latin).

**Verity** truth (Latin).

**Verne, Verna** diminutive forms of Laverne.

**Verona** a variant form of Veronica.

**Veronica** true image (Latin); a variant form is *Verona*; diminutive forms are *Ronnie, Ronny*.

**Veronika** a Scandinavian form of Veronica.

**Veronike** a German form of Veronica.

**Véronique** a French form of Veronica.

**Victoire** a French form of Victoria.

**Victoria** victory (Latin); diminutive forms are *Tory, Vickie, Vita*.

**Vida** beloved (Hebrew); fem form of David.

**Vidya** wisdom, knowledge (Hindu).

**Vilma** a diminutive form of Vilhelmina.

**Vinaya** good behaviour (Hindu).

**Vincentia** fem form of Vincent.

**Viola, Violet** a violet (Latin); a diminutive form is *Vi*.

**Violetta** the Italian form of Viola, Violet.

**Virginia** virginal (Latin); a diminutive form is *Ginnie*.

**Virginie** a Dutch and French form of Virginia.

**Vita** fem form of Vito; a diminutive form of Victoria.

**Vitoria** a Spanish form of Victoria.

**Viv** a diminutive form of Vivien.

**Vivien, Vivienne** fem form of Vivian; a diminutive form is *Viv*.

for the main female character in his play Peter Pan.

**Whitney** a surname and placename, meaning white island or Witta's island, used as a first name (Old English).

**Wilfrida, Wilfreda** fem forms of Wilfrid.

**Wilhelmina, Wilhelmine** fem forms of Wilhelm; diminutive forms are *Elma, Minna, Minnie, Wilma*.

**Willa** fem form of Will, William.

**Williamina** fem form of William.

**Wilma** a diminutive form of Wilhelmina; fem form of William.

**Winifred** joy and peace (Old English); diminutive forms are *Freda, Win, Winnie, Wynn, Wynne*.

**Wynne** a surname, meaning friend, used as a first name; a diminutive form of Winifred.

**Wanda** a variant form of Wenda.

**Wenda** fem form of Wendel; a variant form is *Wanda*.

**Wendy** invented by J. M. Barrie

# X

**Xanthe** yellow (Greek).

**Xaviera** fem form of Xavier.

**Xena, Xene, Xenia** hospitality (Greek).

# Y

**Yasmin, Yasmine** variant forms of Jasmine.

**Yehuda** a variant form of Jehuda.

**Yolanda, Yolande** variant forms of Viola.

**Yseult** an old French form of Isolde.

**Yvette** a diminutive fem form of Yves.

**Yvonne** fem form of Yves.

# Z

**Zabrina** a variant form of Sabrina.

**Zara** flower (Arabic).

**Zelma** a variant form of Selma.

**Zenobia** having life from Zeus (Greek).

**Zinnia** the name of a plant with brightly coloured flowers, used as a first name.

**Zoë, Zoe** life (Greek).

**Zora** dawn (Arabic).

# Top 10
# First Names in England
# and Wales 2001

| Girls | | Boys |
|-------|---|------|
| Chloe | 1 | Jack |
| Emily | 2 | Thomas |
| Megan | 3 | Joshua |
| Jessica | 4 | James |
| Sophie | 5 | Daniel |
| Lauren | 6 | Harry |
| Charlotte | 7 | Samuel |
| Hannah | 8 | Joseph |
| Olivia | 9 | Matthew |
| Lucy | 10 | Lewis |

*Source: Office for National Statistics*

# Top 10
# First Names in Scotland
# 2000

| Girls | | Boys |
|---|:---:|---|
| Chloe | 1 | Jack |
| Amy | 2 | Lewis |
| Lauren | 3 | Ryan |
| Emma | 4 | Cameron |
| Rebecca | 5 | James |
| Megan | 6 | Andrew |
| Caitlin | 7 | Matthew |
| Rachel | 8 | Liam |
| Erin | 9 | Callum |
| Hannah | 10 | Jamie |

*Source: General Register Office for Scotland*

# Top 10
# First Names in N. Ireland
# 2001

| Girls | | Boys |
|---|:---:|---|
| Chloe | ⭐1 | Jack |
| Lauren | ⭐2 | Matthew |
| Emma | ⭐3 | Adam |
| Caitlin | ⭐4 | Ryan |
| Megan | ⭐5 | James |
| Hannah | ⭐6 | Conor |
| Sarah | ⭐7 | Dylan |
| Rebecca | ⭐8 | Joshua |
| Amy | ⭐9 | Thomas |
| Niamh | ⭐10 | Daniel |

*Source: Northern Ireland Statistics & Research Agency*

# Your Little Star

What the future holds for your baby

## ARIES
21 March – 20 April

Aries babies are little firecrackers. They'll demand constant stimulation and even before they learn to talk they'll make sure their voice is heard. Ruled by Mars, these children are fearless. Their innate curiosity and daring makes them quite prone to accidents. They'll do anything for attention and when they start school they are likely to regard grazed knees as battle wounds well won.

When it comes to action, Ariens charge ahead without a thought. Although they are not bullies and tend instead to champion smaller children, they are feared in the playground because of their sheer recklessness. As Ariens grow older they may trample on the feelings of those around them, but they'll be genuinely dismayed by their actions. Not that that will stop them. Young Ariens live by the motto, 'act first, think later'.

Born leaders, Ariens have a knack for motivating other children, though they are usually only out to enlist little helpers for their latest harebrained scheme. Few such schemes ever reach completion, for though Ariens are energetic and full of ideas, they lack perseverance. They'll love active sports like football, but will probably insist on playing all positions: striker, defender and goalkeeper.

**Star names:** Alison, Emma, Neil, Rory, Samuel, Stacy.

## TAURUS
21 April – 20 May

Baby Taureans are a picture of health. They have sturdy legs and a surprisingly strong kick, but they don't usually lash out on a whim. Little Taureans are the models of good behaviour – provided you don't do anything to disturb the peace. With their placid, easy manner, they'll love being tickled, massaged or played gentle music. If they had their way, they'd probably never leave the comfort of their own nursery. Leave them in a strange place or change their diet and they'll start to bellow. It might take a lot to agitate little Taureans but once roused their temper knows no bounds.

Children born under this sign find comfort in routine and they'll kick up a fuss if you attempt to vary their feeding pattern – food is one of their great loves. Music is never far from their minds either. They'll love singing, but don't expect them to perform for the relatives – they hate being pushed into the limelight.

Taureans might seem slow and even lazy at times, but they are simply determined to take life at their own pace. Trying to hurry them will only make them dig their heels in. At school, they might not be the first to write their name, but their ability to concentrate and work steadily enables them to master everything they take on board.

**Star names:** Callum, Christopher, David, Leah, Naomi, Valerie.

## GEMINI
21 May – 21 June

Little Geminians are real bright sparks. Even as they lie in their cot their eyes dart around the room taking everything in. They always wants to be five steps ahead and once they can crawl you'll have to keep a close eye on them. Geminians are full of beans. Restless and inquisitive they are skilled escape artists. If there's a baby who can lift the latch of the stairgate or climb the bars of the playpen, it's this one! Geminians will always want to be in the thick of things and, even as small children, play the part of the social butterfly.

Older Geminians love books, puzzles and computer games. They are full of bright ideas, but skip from one venture to another whenever anything ceases to be a novelty. Children born under this sign are often very clever, but they can fidget and chatter in class. With a great sense of fun and a love of practical jokes, little Geminians will aspire to be the class clown rather than the teacher's pet. Geminians will win you over with their laugh.

No-one can talk like Geminians and they will learn their first words very early on. Expect to have your family secrets aired at the most inopportune moments, but you won't be able to keep a straight face when you tell them off.

**Star names:** Cara, George, Joanne, Joseph, Oliver, Vanessa.

## CANCER
### 22 June – 22 July

With these lovely little babies comes the unwritten sign, 'close family only'. Sudden noises, bright lights and strange faces are likely to terrify them in their first months and they'll cling to the familiar. They'll have a favourite soft toy or rag that they won't let out of their sight, even when they start school. Ruled by the moon, Cancerians could seem moody and changeable. They love cuddles and affection, but rarely show how delighted they are by attention.

Like the crab, little Cancerians tend to retreat into their shell when they feel threatened. Secretive and possessive, they'll want to keep their things under lock and key when they are older. They will tuck away their piggy bank somewhere. Cancerians are very good with money and they're hoarders, too. They love animals, but if you're lucky your toddler will collect dolls or toy cars rather than worms and spiders.

There will be plenty of tears when they start playschool, but Cancerians should do well. They have an aptitude for history, music and art and, while they are not especially keen on sport, as a water sign they will take to swimming. Most of all, they'll love daydreaming about being transported back in time. Stimulate their imagination with stories about the past. **Star names:** Chloe, Iain, Josh, Lucy, Paul, Susan.

## LEO
### 23 July – 22 August

Leos are ruled by the sun – and it shows. They have a wide smile and a warm personality. As long as you are behaving yourself by giving them the attention they deserve they are the very picture of happiness, but say the word 'no' and they'll reveal a very different side. Usually, however, Leos will have tried their charm on you first. They know that when they throw you that winning smile you'll find it difficult to resist.

Leos love being with lots of other babies as long as they're at the centre of the crowd – your toddler will be the life and soul of any party. Leos are born to perform and they're the first to volunteer for school plays. Full of self-confidence, Leos will never question whether any praise they receive is deserved – they know it is.

Any activity with a bit of danger thrown in is great fun for the fearless Leo. They prefer the company of other children to being on their own. When they are bored with their own toys they'll probably swap with their friends and they are always willing to share. School is one big game for these children, but although they are bright they may try to get out of doing their homework. Ask your little Leo to do something and just watch that energy evaporate.

**Star names:** Bethany, Edward, Felix, Georgia, Jane, Richard.

## VIRGO
### 23 August – 23 September

Virgo babies are a pleasure to be around and thrive on routine. Any slight change to the day will be regarded as an unwelcome disruption by these order-loving babies. They have a quiet yet restless and inquisitive nature and are generally fast learners. As soon as they have mastered speech they'll use it to bombard you with those questions they've been bursting to ask.

Virgoans love a peaceful environment – subdued colours, soothing music and relatives who will coo over them endlessly. As they grow older they'll astonish you by tidying their bedroom without being asked and even offering to help with the housework. There'll be no dirty laundry with these children and they won't need much persuasion to jump in the bath or shower. Virgoans hate dirt. They are fusspots and are choosy about their toys and clothes.

Unless encouraged to mingle, children born under this sign can be loners. They love animals and, although they find it difficult to open up with their friends, they'll pamper their pets. If they feel misunderstood they usually resort to sulking. They are studious and bright and don't need to be cajoled into doing their homework – it's already done.

**Star names:** Alistair, Daisy, Jack, Megan, Rachel, William.

## LIBRA
24th September – 22 October

Babies born under this sign adapt quickly to routine. They love soft music and beautiful things – nothing too bold or bright. Libra babies don't need many distractions. They are as happy daydreaming as they are playing with other children. At school their tendency to chatter to anyone who'll listen means they have no problem finding playmates and if there's a squabble going on, they'll always be in the middle trying to sort it out.

It might be difficult to work out whether your little child is lazy or hard-working, quiet or noisy, a leader or follower. That's because as Librans they are composed of opposites. One day they are full of energy, the next all they want to do is sleep. They can also be indecisive to the extreme. Your little Libran will find it impossible to choose between ice-cream or jelly. Ask them what they want for Christmas and they'll change their mind more times than you can count.

With a keen eye for detail, Librans should do well at school. Quick-witted, they know how to charm grown-ups and apply themselves to their goals, but they can be moody when things aren't going to plan. Most of the time, however, your little Libran is great fun to be around **Star names:** Andrew, Charlie, Jamie, Jasmine, Lauren, Tiffany.

## SCORPIO
23 October – 22 November

Little Scorpio babies are so quiet it takes quite some time to work out what's going on in that head of theirs. They are incredibly curious, full of energy and tend to learn very quickly, but although they feel everything intensely they tend to keep their feelings to themselves. Scorpios have endless reserves of energy, but even when they can talk they are no chatterboxes.

With such a vivid imagination, little Scorpios will be scared easily by shadows, horror stories and the dark, but they are not going to let you know that. They are honest about what they think of other people, but extremely secretive when it comes to themselves. They love other people's secrets and will be hooked on ghost stories and mysteries.

Even as babies Scorpio children may suffer from intense jealousy. They need lots of love to feel secure, and can't bear to see affection being lavished on their siblings instead of them. Make them feel loved but don't let jealousy dictate how you divide your attention. Coming last in the egg-and-spoon race is the end of the world and they never forget an injustice. But they are good listeners, honest and loyal to family and friends and will defend them against anything unfair.

**Star names:** Alice, Benjamin, Gary, Heather, Kyle, Peter, Sarah.

## SAGITTARIUS

23 November – 21
December

Little Sagittarians cannot look at a door without wanting to open it. They are born to be free and if they are restless and fretful babies, it's probably because they feel hemmed in. Open the windows, fill the walls with pictures and make sure there's always plenty for them to do. Born explorers, they'll be on their feet in no time and then you'll really find out what it's like to be in five places at once.

Even before they can walk, Sagittarian babies are busy devising their way out of their cot, playpen or nursery. Babies born under this sign are wilful and independent and tend to get themselves into all sorts of mischief just because everything has to be tried once – whether it's sliding down a slide backwards or climbing a tree without knowing how to get down.

As a fire sign, your Sagittarian will be bursting with energy. They would rather be out building jumps for their bicycle than watching telly, but they'll love exciting games and puzzles. Boxes are for opening and food is for throwing – all in good fun, of course. Interested in everyone and everything, they love the company of other children and they'll have lots of friends who will probably be as carefree and mischievous as them.

**Star names:** Aidan, Bridget, Clare, Ethan, James, Philip.

## CAPRICORN
22 December – 20 January

V You can expect lots of bear hugs from these toddlers. As an earth sign, they are strong and affectionate, but also a bit insecure. They need encouragement to join in games with other children, otherwise they'll want to spend all their time reading or talking with grown-ups. Children born under this sign are fascinated by the adult world and, though they need lots of love, they prefer to be treated like a grown-up.

Capricorns have such serious little faces it always seems as if they are in deep concentration, but tickle them and their whole face will light up. They have a great sense of humour and they don't mind if the joke is on them either. They are so funny and have such a kind, caring nature that other children can't help but like them and they'll love playing guardian to smaller playmates.

You'll have hours of fun painting, singing and making things with a Capricorn baby. When they are older they'll enjoy conducting experiments. Capricorns like their routine to be rigidly adhered to. Everything has to be in its proper place. They are not keen on being outdoors or in crowds and once they have established that something is not to their liking, nothing is going to change their mind.

**Star names:** Adam, Cameron, Hannah, Lee.

123

## AQUARIUS

21 January – 19 February

There's nothing that Aquarian babies don't find fascinating. As long as there's something for them to look at they are quite happy. These babies hate to feel stifled, but they like company and will love being in a place where they can watch what you're doing.

The latest interactive toys aren't for Aquarians – they'll soon tire of anything that seems to do all the work for them and are much happier armed with some clothes pegs and some imagination. They'll love playing with building bricks and puzzles. The older Aquarian is often obsessed with taking things to pieces – their room will probably be chaotic. Aquarians are more involved with creative indoor activities than sport and need to be encouraged to play outdoors.

Aquarian toddlers are so original they are sure to stand out from the crowd, but their sense of mischief means they'll have followers whether they like it or not. They love bathtime, travelling in the car and reciting nursery rhymes. Although they like their routine they are also keen to try new things and won't be a problem to feed. Your Aquarian baby hates to feel closed in or restricted and needs to have lots of space to play in.

**Star names:** Aaron, Amy, Daniel, Jake, Katy, Matthew.

Kristian - Kit *
Jocelyn - Joss *
Finn?
Tye *
Keir *
Lottie -
William -

Molly
Lottie
Daisy
Florence - Flo
Matilda - Tilly
Phillippa - Pippa
Morven
Hannah
Jessica
Skye

## PISCES
20 February – 20
March

As a water sign, little Pisceans' faces are more often than not tear-stained. They cry when they are sad, when they are happy and when they are angry. Affectionate to the extreme, they'll shower you with kisses and want you to do the same in return. They expect you to praise their latest painting or song over and over again and feel hurt if you're sharp with them. It's not that Pisceans are vain or attention-seeking – they simply need reassurance that they are doing all right.

Because they are timid, Pisceans take teasing to heart but they are good listeners and like other children – they don't have many problems socialising. They have a desire to heal things so expect them to bring injured creatures into the house. If you have an aching head they'll try to rub it better. They can get too involved in their friends' problems, however, and find it very difficult to say 'no'.

They are born daydreamers and tend to retreat into their world of make-believe when people don't live up to their expectations. They are bright and imaginative and will be enchanted by rainbows, seashells, waterfalls and anything that seems to reinforce their view of the world as a magical place.

**Star names:** Cerys, Colin, Elizabeth, Robert, Rohan, Sophie.